Northumberland County Virginia

Apprenticeships

1750-1852

Compiled by
W. Preston Haynie

HERITAGE BOOKS
2007

HERITAGE BOOKS
AN IMPRINT OF HERITAGE BOOKS, INC.

Books, CDs, and more—Worldwide

For our listing of thousands of titles see our website at
www.HeritageBooks.com

Published 2007 by
HERITAGE BOOKS, INC.
Publishing Division
65 East Main Street
Westminster, Maryland 21157-5026

Copyright © 1994 W. Preston Haynie

Other books by the author:

Northumberland County Bookshelf and Old Books, 1650-1852

Northumberland County, Virginia Apprenticeships, 1650-1750

Records of Indentured Servants and of Certificates for Land, Northumberland County, Virginia, 1650-1795

All rights reserved. No part of this book may be reproduced or transmitted in any form or by any means, electronic or mechanical, including photocopying, recording or by any information storage and retrieval system without written permission from the author, except for the inclusion of brief quotations in a review.

International Standard Book Number: 978-1-55613-947-0

Table of Contents

Preface v

A Background 1

Court Records 11

Court Records of Apprenticeships Overlooked
in Compiling *Northumberland County, Virginia,
Apprenticeships, 1650-1750* 81

Index 84

Preface

The aim of this book is to help one in genealogical research—to aid in tracing family lines and in learning occupations of one's ancestors. Many of the apprenticeship records contain vital information: the name of the child, the name of one or both parents, the name of the person to whom the child was apprenticed, and the trade to be learned. Such information may provide a missing link in doing family research as well as the person's occupation later in life.

Deeds, wills, and birth records usually are the first items researched in family studies. Because many craftsmen did not own land, in many cases deeds will not serve a useful purpose; however, a vital source in genealogical research often has been overlooked—personal property tax records. Since 1782 Virginia has been keeping records of taxes on personal property. Because the information given on the personal property tax lists varies from year to year, they will, for those searching for genealogical clues, be more helpful in some instances than in others. The lists always give the head of the household. In addition, they include the number of white males over the age of 21 and sometimes their names as well. For some years the number of white males between the ages of 16 and 21 is given. Additional information, such as the number of slaves, cattle, horses, and wheels (carriages) may be given.

Unfortunately, these lists are not available in the Northumberland County courthouse or at the Northumberland County Historical Society. The only copies are in the Archives Division of the State Library in Richmond. Unfortunately, also, they are not available on microfilm. These tax records are vital, however, to one having difficulty in establishing family lines during this period.

The court records, for the most part, have been transcribed as they were written. In some cases, a comma or a period has been inserted for clarity, and Record Book (RB) and Order Book (OB) have been abbreviated for brevity. One will notice that a name may be spelled differently within the same document. The word French, for example, is used in Document 162. In the Index the word is France, proving that the two were interchangeable.

My special appreciation goes to the clerk of the court, Steve Thomas, and staff, Linda L. Booth, Eleanor R. Morris, and Emily D. Thomas, for permitting me to occupy a portion of the record room, and to Jim and Joanne Foster, who prepared the manuscript.

A Background

Court records from 1751 to April 1852 indicate a continuation of the institution of apprenticeship that commenced early in the Virginia colony. For a twenty-five year period, the years 1750–1775 had the greatest number of apprenticeships—268. Ranking next were the years 1725–1750, with 183. During the years 1751 to 1852, a number of laws relating to apprenticeships were passed. In November 1769 all bastard children were bound apprentices by the churchwardens of the parish to learn a trade, boys until 21 and girls until 18. The apprentices were to be provided diet, clothes, and lodging, were to be taught to read and write, and at the expiration of the apprenticeship to be paid an allowance equal to that paid indentured servants. The apprentices had access to the court in case of ill usage or failure to be taught a trade.[1]

With the advent of the Revolution, in December 1775, recruiting officers were allowed to recruit apprentices bound under the laws of the colony; however, the master of the apprentice had to give his consent in writing.[2]

During the course of the Revolution, two laws were passed relating to apprentices. The first, passed in October 1780, resulted from the "practice of many tradesmen to entice their apprentices to enlist as soldiers, and to sell them as substitutes for large sums of money."[3] Because of this practice every tradesman found guilty, if over the age of 50, had to pay double the amount of money taken, one portion going to the informer and the other part going to the commonwealth, "to be applied as a bounty to enlist soldiers in the continental army."[4] If the offender was under the age of 50 and was convicted before a courtmartial, he was to serve as part of the state's quota of continental troops.[5]

The second law, passed the same month, provided that at least half of the male orphans who lived below the falls of the respective rivers in the eastern part of the commonwealth "be bound to the sea."[6] Because the trades to be learned are not mentioned in many cases of orphans being apprenticed, one does not know how many orphans from Northumberland County were apprenticed to the sea. A review of those serving in the navy during the Revolution may be of some help. Well before the Revolution, in 1758, Thomas Robinson was bound to John Heath to learn the art of a sailor (Document 72). Well after the Revolution, in 1830, William Ashburn, orphan of Haynie Ashburn,

---

1. William Waller Hening, *The Statutes at Large* (Richmond: Whittet and Shepperson, 1969), vol. 8, 376.
2. Ibid., vol. 9, 81.
3. Ibid., vol. 10, 335.
4. Ibid., 336.
5. Ibid.
6. Ibid., 385.

was bound to Hiram Ingram to learn the art of a mariner (Document 397).

A law of October 1785 was similar in many ways to laws passed before the Revolution. Every orphan who did not have an estate sufficient to maintain him or her out of the profits was, by order of the court, bound an apprentice until the age of 21, if a boy, or 18, if a girl, to learn a trade. Apprentices also could be bound by their fathers after the age of 16 to serve until 24 or any shorter time. Another law passed the same year allowed for courts to receive complaints of apprentices against their masters for insufficient food, clothing, or lodging, or for ill usage.[7]

Also in October 1785, the General Assembly directed the courts of each county the following March to divide each county into districts. An election was then to be held "consisting of freeholders and householders only for the purpose of chusing [choosing] three discreet, fit, and proper persons, being freeholders of and residents within the same, who shall be called and denominated overseers of the poor."[8] Some counties in the state had replaced churchwardens with overseers of the poor as early as 1780; however, in the more conservative Northumberland, the first poor or orphans bound out by the overseers of the poor was October 9, 1786 (Document 316). Sally Popperwell, on February 13, 1786, was the last person to be bound out by the churchwardens (Document 311).

The year 1792 saw a number of provisions in laws passed similar to those enacted before the Revolution: any guardian, with the approval of the court, could bind his ward to learn a trade; county courts could receive complaints of apprentices; and bastard children were bound apprentices by the overseers of the poor.[9]

An act passed by the General Assembly on January 19, 1805, contained two provisions relating to apprentices bound to learn the trade of a seaman. The first stated that if any apprentice should desert the vessel on which he had been placed, without the consent of his master, it was lawful for any justice of the peace of any county, upon the complaint of the master, to arrest him and commit him to the jail of his county. The apprentice was to remain there until the vessel was ready for its voyage or until the master requested his discharge.[10] The second provision addressed the rights of the apprentice seaman; if he could offer sufficient proof to the justice of the peace that he had been treated cruelly and forced to remain aboard the ship, it was lawful for the justice to discharge him.[11]

In a number of cases, apprentices did register complaints with the county court. It is rather remarkable that the apprentices were aware of their rights and

---

7. Ibid., vol. 12, 197, 198.
8. Ibid., 27.
9. Samuel Shepherd, *Statutes at Large of Virginia* (Richmond: Printed by Samuel Shepherd, 1835), vol. 1, 105, 106, 120.
10. Ibid., vol. 3, 128.
11. Ibid., 129.

the procedures for making grievances. On the other hand, one does not know the number of apprentices who were too shy to register complaints and consequently suffered abuse or inadequate food, lodging, or clothing. Ezekiel Coffee, an apprentice to Charles James, applied to the court to be discharged. The court agreed that he had served his time and was discharged (Document 124). Likewise, the court agreed that Henage Sebastian was of full age and should be discharged from his master, George Astain (Document 248). On the other hand, the court ruled that Robuck Hudson, an apprentice to George Haynie, had not served his full time and was to remain with his master for thirty-three more days (Document 163).

The most frequent complaint of apprentices was of ill usage. Mary Walker petitioned the court against Francis Roles for ill usage of her son, John Burros. The court cautioned Roles to give better treatment or Burros would be discharged from his service (Document 142). Five months later, after hearing witnesses of each party, the court did discharge Burros from Roles (Document 147). On the same day, the churchwardens of St. Stephens parish were ordered to bind out John Burros according to law (Document 148). Josiah Gaskins complained to the court against John Betts for ill usage. The court, after hearing each party, ordered Betts to give security for his good behavior for one year. Betts refused and was committed to jail until such security be given (Document 251). Joseph Hudnall, an apprentice to Richard Thomas, complained to the court; however, Thomas did not appear and the complaint was to be heard at the next court (Document 255). On the motion of Thomas Gaskins, an apprentice to James Lewis, the court ordered the sheriff to summon Lewis for ill usage to appear at the next court (Document 265). At the next court the complaint was heard and dismissed (Document 266). Abraham Dunaway, an apprentice to Thomas Thomas to learn the trade of a tailor, was discharged from Dunaway after nine months because of ill usage (Document 320).

In addition to ill treatment, apprentices resorted to the court for other reasons. Winifred Walker, orphan of John Walker, petitioned the court for dues allowed her. Jane Humphris, to whom Winifred had been apprenticed, and Joseph Hudnall, her security, were ordered to pay Winifred three pounds ten shillings and court costs (Document 318). For reasons not given in the court document, John Sank, who had been bound to Peter Adams to learn the trade of a house carpenter, came into court and, with the approval of Adams, was bound, by the overseers of the poor, to Lucius S. Winstead to learn the trade of a blacksmith (Document 414). William Seebrie agreed that he would discharge Patrick Carrold from his service and pay him four pounds ten shillings on the condition that Patrick would excuse him from teaching him the trade of a cooper (Document 1). John Kessady, a poor orphan who had been bound to Thomas Taylor, was sold or turned over to some other person contrary to law. The court ordered the overseers of the poor of Wicomico parish to bind the orphan to a proper person until he reached 21 (Document 365).

Apprentices were paid freedom dues at the expiration of their time of service, boys when they reached 21 and girls, 18. In most cases, the documents simply state that the person to whom the boy or girl is being apprenticed is to pay his or her freedom dues according to law. William Seebrie agreed to pay Patrick Carrold four pounds ten shillings (Document 1). The court ordered that the overseers of the poor of Wicomico parish bind out John Cessaty and that his master pay him $20 at the expiration of his apprenticeship (Document 357). The master of James Adams, also of Wicomico parish, was to pay Adams $10 at the end of his term (Document 358). Giles Boggess, orphan of Bennett Boggess, at the age of 17 was bound to Richard Crute until he became 21 to learn the trade of a shop joiner. In lieu of his freedom dues, he was to receive a broadcloth suit, a shirt, shoes, etc. (Document 21).

Some orphans had sufficient estates to maintain them; others did not. One example of an orphan not having an estate sufficient to maintain him is Burgess Pitman. As a result of his having such a small estate, John F. Fallin and Isaac Bayse were appointed to bind Burgess to Fortunatus Pitman (Document 342).

With the beginning of the Revolution, a preponderance of those apprenticed were orphans. To the dismay of genealogists, one will notice that in many cases the names of parents are not given. Probably because of a strong belief in the Puritan work ethic, on September 12, 1796, the court ordered six idle boys to be bound apprentices (Document 360). Although they were poor, the court document does not state whether they were orphans. An increasing number of free blacks and mulattos also were being apprenticed during that period.

Although one might think the number of young boys apprenticed to become tailors, carpenters and joiners, and shoemakers to be excessive, every community had its tradesmen. Not until after the Revolution could local craftsmen satisfy the demand for goods. As a result, skilled craftsmen received good wages for their products; in fact, many colonists found it as cheap or cheaper to buy items from England. Joseph Ball, in a letter of his *Journal* to Joseph Chinn of Morattico, Lancaster County, Virginia, states that he is not sending any clothing to his Negroes because he has been told there are great quantities of goods now going over and very likely Chinn can buy them cheaper in the colony than he could send them. (Chinn is looking after the business affairs of Ball's several plantations in Virginia.)[12] Rawleigh Downman, who married the daughter of Joseph Ball, in a letter from England in 1765 just prior to his return to Virginia, states that he intends to bring some clothes for his people, another indication that clothes were as expensive or maybe even more expensive in the colony.[13] After his return, Downman continued to order goods from England for his Negroes, as well as material, shoes, and stockings for his family.[14]

One would have to make a careful study to determine how many of the apprentices continued in their trades at the end of their apprenticeships. To make such a study for one individual would be less time consuming. George

---

12. *Letter Journal of Joseph Ball and Rawleigh Downman*, Manuscript Division, Library of Congress, 226.
13. Ibid., 241.
14. Ibid., 247.

Haynie, for example, was apprenticed to William Eskridge at 16 to learn the trade of a joiner and house carpenter.[15] He continued in this trade as long as he remained in Northumberland County. Betweeen 1756 and 1770, he also had six apprentices bound to him to learn the trade of house carpenter and joiner. One of these was his own brother, William Haynie (Document 46).

The Roger Jones Family Papers contain a statement from George Haynie to Thomas Jones. This statement provides an idea of work a carpenter would have done during this period. Thomas Jones served as clerk of Northumberland County from 1749/50 to 1778 and lived at Mt. Zion. The schoolhouse mentioned in the statement, although badly in need of repair, is still standing.

May 1761   Thomas Jones to George Haynie

	£	s	d
To getting of 7 thousand 2 hundred & thirty at 6/ p^r thousand		2	3	3
To nailing on 10 Squair [square] and a half at 6/ p^r Squair [square]		3	3
To puting [putting] up 56 feet Cornish at the old house at 2^d p^r foot			9	4
To building the house of office	3		
To a small clausett [closet] at the old house & one window & 8 Lights & a door			11
To 1 Batten Door 6/ To fasing [facing] two windows up stares [stairs] 2/			8
To 1 Close stool & a child's small chair			4
To a Bedstead 5/. to Caseing [casing] of a Coffin 5/.			10
To gitting [getting] of two hundred Boards from the stump & nail^g them on			7	6
To gitting [getting] five hundred D^o to nailing on the chitching [kitchen] & stable			18	6
To proping [propping] the stable & mak^g 4 Stauls [stalls] to mak^g a Door to the same			10
To gitting [getting] a frame to the chitching [kitchen] & Laths for the Chimney			6
To mak^g a tan fatt [fat] 10/. to a Large gate & frame 10/.	1		
To Repairing the old house of Broun's to mak^g 1 Door 6/ 2 window shetters [shuttters] 3/ to mending the floor & 2 Doors 5/			14
To Triming [trimming] a Cannoe [canoe] & making of two Ores [oars] 10/			10
To making 4 oars for the boat 6/ 1 spring for the Rid^g Chair 2/			8

---

15. Order Book 1743–49, Northumberland County, 416.

To mak^g a small Walnut Coffin 10/. to mak^g large table & chest		1	10
To mending 2 oval tables & 12 Mahogany chairs			4
To gitt^g [getting] of Boards & mak^g a funnell [funnel] to your chitching [kitchen]			5
To making of Six Wheel Barrows at 2/6 p^r D^o			15
To making of a burd [bird] chage [cage] 12/6 to repair^g one old gate			15
To mend^g a frame of a Looking glass 6^d to mak^g a horse tumbler 7/6			8
To Build^g of a Bee house 9/ to 4 wheel Barrows at 2/6 p^r			19
To guinting [?] and laying down 124 foot of plank at the old schoolhouse		2	6
To sawing of white oak plank & puting [putting] it on the pair head of your mill		12	6
To mak^g a Pole for your Riding Chair		3	
To a Large chest that you bought of me	1		
To 4 hundred 4 penny nails & an Ink stand that you had of me		5	
To work done on Building of your Mill house		10	
To Building & moveing [moving] the Lattin [Latin] school	15		
To Building your Barn	27		
To Build^g you a small house for your Clarke [clerk] office	3		
To D^o a stable at the home house taken from the stump	25		
To D^o a store house	6		
To D^o a Meat house	3	10	
To D^o your Dwelling house from the stump	65		
	167	01	7

E.E. p^r me George Haynie
March 19 day 1776[16]

In addition to the Jones papers, court records reveal additional information about George Haynie. On May 12, 1764, the county court directed that he be paid two hundred pounds of tobacco for setting up sign boards.[17] In 1766 he was, by the court, appointed guardian to Mosely Mott, orphan of Mosely Mott. In the same year Mott was, by the court, bound an apprentice to Haynie[18] (Document 170). On April 12, 1768, the court ordered that James Craine pay unto George Haynie fifty pounds of tobacco for two days attendance at court as a witness for him at the suit of John Efford.[19]

---

16. Papers of the Jones Family, Microfilm Shelf No. 18,063, contents 20–21.
17. Order Book 1762–66, Part 2, 431.
18. Ibid., 460.
19. Order Book, 1767–70, 190.

There is no evidence that George Haynie owned land until he bought a half acre from Rodham Kenner and his wife, Sally, on May 28, 1773.[20] In 1776, George Haynie and his wife, Catherine, sold one acre of land to Winifred Berry.[21] It is believed he and his family left the county shortly thereafter. Another rather extensive statement among the Jones family papers is one of Thomas Thomas, a tailor. Abraham Dunaway was apprenticed to Thomas on October 9, 1786, to learn the trade of a tailor, but was discharged June 11, 1787, upon the complaint of Dunaway (Documents 314, 320). The statement is of interest because it reveals the work a tailor did at this period in history.

1775		Mr Thomas Jones Dr to Thomas Thomas	£	s	d
Janry	5th	To Buttoning half trimm'd green waiscoat for Catesby			7 $^{1}/_{2}$
	10th	To Mending and Making new cuffs to an old Coat		2	
	12th	To Buttoning a Pair of Breeches			6
Feb.	6th	To Putting new lining & Pockets to pr of Blue Breeches		2	
	8th	To Making a suit of half trimm'd Uniforms son Thos	1	6	
	13	To putting new sleeves to, and mending a Coat son Bathurst		1	6
		To making a Pair of Russia Drill spatter dashes		2	6
	28	To Making a Pair of Breeches for son Merriwether		2	6
Mar	6th	To Strapping, new lining & Pocketing, pr of blue breeches		2	3
	10th	To a pr of Breeches for son Catesby		1	6
	18th	To Mending a new market coat		1	
	20th	To Mending & Strapping pr of Breeches for son Thomas		1	6
	24th	To Making a half trimm'd Uniform'd Coat for Catesby		16	
		To Work done to a white Cloth Waiscoat for Do		1	6
		Rec'd by note to Mr Daniel Muse's		12	
			2	9	4 $^{1}/_{2}$
		Rec'd of son Catesby 1 Bottle of snuff		2	
			2	7	4 $^{1}/_{2}$

---

20. Record Book 9, Part 1, 300–302.
21. Ibid., Part 2, 640.

1775	Col. Thomas Jones to Thos Thomas				
	To sundries as by Bill Drawn		2	7	4
May					
4	To Mending a Jeans coat of Robert Snape			1	3
21	To Making Brown Holland Coat for Bathurst			2	6
24	To Making Brown Holland Coat for Merriwether			3	
June					
13	To Making a Jeans coat & waiscoat for self			12	6
28	To Making p^r of fustien Breeches for Ambrose			2	
July					
8	To making a Hunting Cap for Catesby			2	6
	To Making 2 Waiscoats 2 p^r of Breeches of B				
	Linnen [linen] p^r Mansfield			6	
	To Making a p^r of Brown Holland Breeches				
	for self			2	6
	To Making a p^r of Russia Drill Breeches				
	for Bathurst			2	
	To Altering a p^r of Brown Holland Breeches				
	for Catesby				6
	To Making a p^r of Brown Holland Breeches				
	for Catesby				6
Augst					
18	To Making a p^r of Brown Holland Breeches				
	for self			2	6
	To Making a camblet cloat for Catesby			10	
Oct^r					
20	To Making a Coat for Bathurst			3	
	To Making Bath Beaver Coat & Waist^t bound				
	holes & Edges for self			12	6
	To Mending 2 p^r of Buckskin breeches for				
	Ambrose & Billy			1	6
Nov					
5	To Mending a Hussar & Great Coat			2	
	To Making a p^r of Blue Breeches for Bathurst			2	
10	To Making a Green coat for Plato			3	6
30	To Making a Coat & Waist^t with bound holes				
	& edges for Merriwether			6	
	To putting new sleeves to an old coat for				
	Bathurst			1	3
		6	19	4 $^1/_2$	
			3	6	
		6	15	10 $^1/_2$	

Mrs Jones

Sept			
20	To Making a pr of Trowsers [trousers] for Merriwether	1	
	To Making 2 pr of Ditto for Bathurst	1	6
	To Making a Coat for Bathurst	1	6
	To Making a pr of Breeches for Billy	1	3
	To Mending a great coat & putting buttons to spatter dashes Billy	1	3
		6	6[22]

For some of those apprentices, it is not certain whether after their apprenticeship they continued with the trade for which they were bound. The life of a tradesman was better than that of an indentured servant or common laborer but not as good as that of a professional or planter. The lower and middle classes of Virginia, as well as the more well-to-do, placed much value on the education of children. One such example from the middle or upper class being apprenticed to learn a trade is Rodham Kenner Cralle, who was bound to William Grayson on January 9, 1769, to learn the trade of a carpenter and joiner (Document 207). The son of Rodham Kenner Cralle and Elizabeth Straughan, he was bound by the court. Although the document does not mention that he was bound with the consent of his mother, one can assume this to be true, and that she was looking after the interest of her son. The will of the elder Cralle was probated on March 9, 1761.[23] Elizabeth subsequently married (2) George Harvey, (3) Jeremiah Middleton, and (4) Charles Haynie. She was married to Middleton at the time her son was apprenticed.

In 1774 Elizabeth Middleton, the widow of Rodham Kenner Cralle and the mother of Rodham Kenner Cralle, gave, by deed of gift, 186 acres to her two sons, Rodham Kenner and William Taite, reserving for herself use of the land during her natural life. On December 7, 1776, for fifty pounds she conveyed the land to her son Rodham Kenner, William Taite being deceased.[24] On the same day, Rodham Kenner sold the land to Peter Cox for two hundred pounds.[25] Rodham Kenner, in turn, bought 86 acres from Cox for two hundred pounds.[26] On October 14, 1782, Rodham Kenner leased 86 acres from Charles Haynie, who possessed the land as a result of his intermarriage with Elizabeth Middleton, mother of Rodham Kenner. The land belonged to Elizabeth during her natural life and during the natural life of Haynie. Upon the decease of either, the lease

---

22. Papers of the Jones Family, contents 20–21.
23. Record Book 5, 353.
24. Record Book 10, 81.
25. Ibid., 85.
26. Ibid., 158.

was to be void.[27] During this period, Cralle appears to have been farming the 86 acres he owned and the 86 acres he leased from Haynie. One does not know whether he was also following his trade as a carpenter and joiner. Like many of the early colonists, he may have been involved in a number of adventures. On November 29, 1786, Cralle and his wife, Catherine, sold the 86 acres that he bought from Cox to Stephen Self Jr. for eighty pounds.[28]

During the Revolution, Cralle served as a private and sergeant in various Virginia regiments of the Continental Line. In 1789 he was living in Frederick County, Virginia.[29] Cralle may have moved west because so much of the land in the eastern part of the state was worn out by the raising of tobacco or he may have been in search of better opportunities.

Court records of apprenticeships from 1751 to April 1852 reveal a tremendous change in the institution of apprenticeship. The years 1750 to 1775 witnessed the greatest number being apprenticed of any twenty-five year period. Some of these were poor and were bound by the churchwardens. Others were orphans, although in many cases this term is misleading to the modern reader. The dictionary defines orphan as "a child who has lost both parents through death, or less commonly, one parent."[30] During this period in history, the latter is frequently true. Elizabeth, the mother of Rodham Kenner Cralle, is still living when he is apprenticed (Document 207). In most cases when one parent is deceased, it is the father. This period before the Revolution also saw a number of children from large middle-class families being apprenticed after reaching the age of 14 or 16.

The most drastic changes in the institution of apprenticeship occurred after the Revolution. In 1786 the overseers of the poor assumed the responsibilities formerly held by the churchwardens in binding out the poor. The nation, the state, and the county, as well, faced a host of problems; chief among these were financial difficulties. On October 12, 1795, the overseers of the poor of Wicomico parish returned a report that they had no balance in their hands. The lower district of St. Stephens parish made the same statement.[31] Similar reports were to be given in subsequent years. The period following the Revolution saw more poor and orphans being apprenticed. The county, as well as the state, was floundering for a system of education. The period saw fewer sons of middle and upper classes being apprenticed. For those who were, the documents or indentures, usually witnessed by the father, mother, or guardian, the apprentice, and the person to whom he was being apprenticed, are rather lengthy.

---

27. Record Book 11, 301.
28. Record Book 14, 24.
29. James F. Lewis Collection, Northumberland County Historical Society.
30. *The Random House College Dictionary* (New York: Random House, Inc., 1973).
31. Order Book 1790–95, 579.

Court Records

1. 14 Jan. 1750/51—William Seebrie agrees with his servant Patrick Carrold that he will discharge him from his service and pay him four pounds ten shillings upon condition that the said Patrick will excuse him from learning him the trade of a cooper as was agreed between the Parties sometime past. *OB 1749–53, 116.*

2. 14 Jan. 1750/51—Manly Brown Orphan of Thomas Brown deced is by the Court bound to John Smith till he arrives to the age of twenty one years, the said Smith is to learn him the trade of a Turner as also to Read, Write and Cypher [cipher] and pay him his freedom dues according to Law—Whereupon he together with Winfield Wright his Security entered into and acknowledged Bond for the due of the Same in the Penalty of 10,000 Pounds Tob°. *OB 1749–53, 116.*

3. 13 May 1751—Patience Berry Orphan of Thomas Berry deceased aged eleven years is by the Court Bound to William Berry till she arives [arrives] to the age of eighteen years. The said Berry is to learn her to Read, write, sew and Spin and pay her her freedom dues according to Law. Charles Coppedge entering himself Security for the due Performance of the Same in the Penalty of ten thousand Pounds of Tob°. *OB 1749–53, 159.*

4. 13 May 1751—Mary Appleby orphan of John Appleby deceased aged about ten years is by the Court bound to John McGoon till she arives [arrives] to the age of eighteen years. The said McGoon is to learn her to Read, write, sew and Spin & pay her her freedom dues according to Law. John Gaskins entering himself Security for the due Performance of the Same in the Penalty of ten thousand Pounds of Tobacco. *OB 1749–53, 159.*

5. 13 May 1751—James Hill Orphan of Luke Hill deceased is by the Court bound to Robt Palmer till he arrives to the age of twenty one years and the said Palmer is to learn him to read, write and the trade of a Shoemaker and pay him his freedom dues according to law. Whereupon Moses Lunsford entered himself Security for the due performance of the Same in the Penalty of ten thousand Pounds of Tob°. *OB 1749–53, 163.*

6. 15 May 1751—Mary Berry Orphan of Thomas Berry deced is by the Court Bound to William Lunsford till she arrives to the age of eighteen years— The said Lunsford is to learn her to read, write, sew and Spin and at the Expiration of her time pay her her freedom dues according to Law—Whereupon George Oldham entered himself Security for the due Performance of the Same in the Penalty of 5000£ Tobacco. *OB 1749–53, 191.*

7. 10 July 1751—Susana Mays Orphan of Henry Mayes deced is by the Court bound to John Wood till she arives [arrives] to the age of 18 years. The said Wood is to learn her to Read the Bible, Sew and Spin and at the Expiration of her time pay her her freedom dues according to Law, Whereupon Thomas Cotrell & Thomas Bridgman entering themselves his Securities for the due performance of the same in five thousand pounds of Tob^o. *OB 1749–53, 211.*

8. 10 July 1751—Jemimah Nash Orphan of Robert Nash deced is by the C^t [Court] bound to John Taylor Junr till she arives [arrives] to the age of 18 years and the said Taylor is to Learn her to read the Bible & sew & Spin and at the Expiration of her time pay her her freedom dues according to Law, Whereupon Richd Hudnall & David Lattimore entering themselves his Securities for the due performance of the Same in five thousand pounds of Tob^o. *OB 1749–53, 211.*

9. 10 July 1751—Anne Bell Orphan of William Bell deced is by the Court bound to Stephen Hall till she arives [arrives] to the age of eighteen years. The said Hall is to learn her to read, write, sew & spin and at the Expiration of her time pay her her Freedom dues according to Law. Whereupon Lewis Lamkin & James Lewis entered themselves Securities for the due Performance of the Same in the Penalty of 5000 pounds of Tob^o. *OB 1749–53, 213.*

10. 9 Sept. 1751—Richard Tossett orphan of Richard Tossett deced. is by the Court bound to John Sebrie till he arrives to the age of twenty one years, the said Seebrie is to learn him the art and mystery of a shoemaker and to read and write and at the expiration of his time pay him his Freedom dues according to Law, Whereupon James Marsh and William Seebrie entered themselves securities for the due Performance of the same in the Penalty of five thousand pounds of Tobacco. *OB 1749–53, 221.*

11. 10 Feb. 1752—Charles Haynie orphan of Ormsby Haynie deced is by the Court bound to Isaac Beachem till he arrives to the age of twenty one years. The said Beachem is to Learn him the Trade of a house carpenter and to find him sufficient cloathing [clothing], Lodging & Diet during the Term aforesaid and at the Expiration of the said Term to pay him his freedom dues according to Law. Whereupon James Crain & Robert Middleton entered themselves securities in the Penalty of 10,000 pounds of Tob^o for the due performance of the same. *OB 1749–53, 252.*

12. 10 Feb. 1752—Corbell Hill orphan of Luke Hill deceased is by the Court bound to Richard Alverson till he arives [arrives] to the age of twenty one years, the said Alverson is to Learn him the trade of a Shoemaker and to Read and Write and at the Expiration of the said time pay him his freedom dues according to Law. Whereupon Samuel Blackwell gent. becoming his Security for the due Performance of the same in the Penalty of ten thousand pounds of Tob^o. *OB*

1749–53, 252.

13. 10 Feb. 1752—Anne and Susanna Vanlandingham are by the Court bound to Jane Lamkin till they arrive to the age of eighteen years. The said Lamkin is to Learn them to read, write, sew, spin etc. and at the expiration of the aforesaid Time pay them their freedom dues according to Law, Whereupon Samuel Eskridge & James entered themselves Securities for the due Performance of the same in the Penalty of ten thousand pounds of Tobacco. *OB 1749–53, 253.*

14. 13 April 1752—John Cox Orphan of William Cox deced is by the Court bound to Elisha Snow till he arives [arrives] to the age of twenty one years. The said Snow is to Learn him the trade of a Joyner [joiner] & House Carpenter and to Read and Write and pay him his Freedom dues according to Law. Whereupon Francis Timberlake entered himself Security for the due Performance of the same in the Penalty of ten thousand pounds of Tob°. *OB 1749–53, 269.*

15. 11 May 1752—Jane Carty orphan of John Carty deced. is by the Court bound to John Blincoe till she arrives to the age of eighteen years. The said Blincoe is to learn her to read, sew and spin and at the expiration of the aforesaid term to pay her her freedom dues according to Law. Whereupon Samuel Eskridge & James Lewis entered themselves his securities for the due performance of the same in the Penalty of five thousand pounds of Tob°. *OB 1749–53, 278.*

16. 8 June 1752—Richard Thomas Orphan of Richard Thomas deced is by the Court bound to Isaac Beachem who is to Learn him the trade of a House Carpenter and to read and write and at the Expiration of his time to pay him his freedom dues According to Law. Whereupon Thomas Brown entered himself Security for the due Performance of the Same in the Penalty of five thousand pounds of Tob°. *OB 1749–53, 300.*

17. 8 June 1752—Diane Smith Orphan of Samuel Smith deced eleven years old in July last is by the Court bound To Thomas Harcum till she arives [arrives] to the age of eighteen. The said Thomas is to Learn her to Read, Write, Sew and Spinn [spin] & at the Expiration of the aforesaid Term to pay her her freedom dues according to Law. Whereupon William Barrott entered himself Security for the due Performance of the same in the Penalty of five thousand pounds of Tob°. *OB 1749–53, 301.*

18. 10 Aug. 1752—William Edwards orphan of Ralph Edwards deced. is by the Court bound to William Ashburn till he arrives to the age of twenty one years. The said Ashburn is learn him to read and write and the trade of a Taylor [tailor] and at the expiration of the aforesaid Term to pay him his freedom dues according to Law. Whereupon John Humphries and Spencer Haynie entered themselves securities for due performance of the same in Penalty 5,000 Pounds of Tobacco. *OB 1749–53, 332.*

19. 9 Oct. 1752—Sarah Harper Orphan of John Harper deceased is by the Court Bound to Joseph Ball till she arives [arrives] to the age of Eighteen years (she being now Twelve years old). The said Ball is to learn her to Read, Write, sew and Spinn [spin] and at the Expiration of the said Term the said Ball is to pay her her freedom dues according to Law, whereupon George Ball Entered himself Security with the said Joseph for the due Performance of the same in the Penalty of Five thousand Pounds of Tobacco. *OB 1749–53, 360.*

20. 13 Nov. 1752—Ordered that the Churchwardens of Wicomico Parish bind out the orphans of Samuel Mahanes [Mahane] deceased according to Law. *OB 1749–53, 365.*

21. 14 May 1753—Giles Boggess Orphan of Bennett Boggess Deced, the age of Seventeen Years the Eighth Day of July next, is by the Court Bound to Richard Crute till he arives [arrives] to the age of Twenty one Years. In Consideration that the said Crute is to Learn him the Trade of a Shop Joiner and at the Expiration of the Servitude to give him a Suit of Broad Cloath [cloth] Clothes, a Shirt, Shoes etc. in lieu of his freedom dues. Whereupon the said Crute together with James Blincoe & Samuel Eskridge his Securities bind themselves in the Penalty of Five thousand Pounds of Tobacco each for the due Performance of the same. *OB 1749–53, 403.*

22. 10 Sept. 1753—James Harrison an Infant of the age of Nine Years next January Orphan of Thomas Harrison deced is by the Court bound to Charles James till he arives [arrives] to the age of Twenty one Years. In Consideration whereof the said Charles James is to learn him the Trade of a Weaver, to Read and Write and at the Expiration of the aforesaid Term to pay him his freedom dues according to Law. For the due performance of which the said Charles James together with William Barrett jun. his Security bind themselves in the Penalty of Five thousand Pounds of Tobacco. *OB 1753–56, 50.*

23. 10 Sept. 1753—Ordered that the Churchwardens of St Stephens Parish bind out William Todd orphan of Cornelus Todd deced according to Law. *OB 1753–56, 51.*

24. 10 Sept. 1753—Thomas Hill (orphan of Ezekiel Hill deced) of the age of nine years the 15th Day of August last is by the Court bound to John James till he arives [arrives] to the age of twenty one years. In Consideration the said John James is to learn him the Trade of a Turner, to Read, Write and at the Expiration of his Service to pay him his freedom dues according to Law for the performance of which the said John James together with John Hudnall and William Cook his Securities bind themselves in the Penalty of Five thousand Pounds of Tobacco. *OB 1753–56, 53.*

25. 12 Nov. 1753—Ordered that the Churchwardens of St Stephens Parish bind out Joshua Murphey, John Campbell, Mary Doolan, John Patridge & William [unreadable] Thomas according to Law. *OB 1753–56, 57.*

26. 12 Nov. 1753—Ordered that the Executor of John Oldham jun^r deced pay unto Thomas Betts his freedom dues according to Law. *OB 1753–56, 64.*

27. 11 Feb. 1754—William Astin & Valentine Astin Orphans of John Astin deced are by the Court bound Apprentices to Benjamin Foster until they shall respectively attain to the age of Twenty one years. In consideration of which the said Benjamin Foster is to learn them both the Trade of a Bricklayer and to Read, Write and Cypher and at the Expiration of their Apprenticeships to pay them each their freedom dues according to Law. For the due performance of which the said Benjamin Foster together with Adcock Hobson and John Rout his Securities bind themselves in the Penalty of Ten thousand pounds of Tobacco. *OB 1753–56, 76.*

28. 8 April 1754—Judy Care Orphan of Thomas Care deced is by the Court bound an apprentice to George Pickren till she arives [arrives] to the age of Eighteen years, she being of the Age of Six Years the 27th Day of May last. In consideration whereof the said Pickren is to learn her to Read, Sew & Spin and to pay her her freedom dues according to Law. For the due Performance of which the said George Pickren together with George McGoon & John Wood his Securities bind themselves in the Penalty of Five thousand Pounds of Tobacco. *OB 1753–56, 99.*

29. 13 May 1754—Winefred Railey orphan of Daniel Railey deced. is by the Court bound to John Parry till she arrives to the age of eighteen years. In consideration the said Parry is to cause her to be learned to read, sew & spin & at the expiration of her service to pay her her freedom dues according to Law. For the due performance of which the said Parry with John Taylor & John Swift his Securities each acknowledged themselves to be bound in the Penalty of Five thousand Pounds of Tobacco. *OB 1753–56, 138.*

30. 13 May 1754—James Harvey Orphan of James Harvey deced is by the Court bound to William Johnston till he arives [arrives] to the age of Twenty one years. In consideration that the said Johnston is to learn him or cause him to be learned the Trade of a Tight Cooper & to Read, Write & Cypher [cipher] and at the Expiration of his Service to pay him his freedom dues according to Law. For the due performance of which the said William Johnston together with Samuel Downing & [page worn] Connor his Securities bind themselves in the Penalty of [page worn] thousand pounds of Tobacco. *OB 1753–56, 139.*

31. 9 July 1754—Order'd that the Churchwardens of St Stephens parish for the time being bind out Jane Barrett daughter of William Barrett according to law. *OB 1753–56, 166.*

32. 27 Sept. 1754—Will of John Conway . . . my will and desire that my son Robert have eight years schooling and then bound to some handy craft trade untill [until] he shall attain ye age of twenty years. . . . *RB 3, 242.*

33. 13 Jan. 1755—An Indenture of apprenticeship between John Hornsby an Infant under the age of twenty one years by William Baysie his guardian and William Anderson was acknowledged by the parties & admitted to record. *OB 1753–56, 253.* [John Hornsby was the son of John Hornsby. *OB 1753–56, 362.*]

34. 13 Jan. 1755—This Indenture made this 13th day of Jany in the year of our Lord one thousand seven hundred and fifty five Between John Hornsby of the County of Northumberland an Infant under the guardianship of William Baysie of the one part and William Anderson of the County of Westmoreland Shop Joyner [joiner] of the other part Witnesseth that the above said John Hornsby by and with the advice and Consent of his said guardian for & In Consideration of the above said William Anderson learning him the said John Hornsby the art and Trade of a Shop Joyner [joiner] Hath Voluntarily bound himself and [an] apprentice unto the above said William Anderson To Serve him the said William Anderson in all and every lawful Calling and Employment that he the said William Anderson shall order or direct him the said John Hornsby—Provided he the said William Anderson not keep him the said John Hornsby from the Trade so much as to Prevent or Hinder him of learning his Designed Art or Trade—and further the said John Hornsby and his above said guardian does [do] agree to and with the above said William Anderson that he the said William may take the said John Hornsby from his Trade at any time to assist and help to tend Cows any or every year between the Date hereof and ye expiration of his apprenticeship without Impeachment of Hinderance [hindrance] to him the said John Hornsby's learning the Trade above said and further the said John Hornsby does firmly Posetively [positively] agree with the above said William Anderson to furnish and keep the said John in good and Sufficient Cloaths [clothes] for the two first years ensuing the Date hereof at their own expence [expense] that he the said John shall faithfully and at all times obey and keep all the said William Anderson's lawful commands and Act and Do in all things as a faithful Apprentice ought to do In Witness whereof they have hereunto set their Hands and fixt [fixed] their Seals the Day and Year above written.

Signed Sealed and Delivered   John Hornsby
in presence of   William Bayse
        The Court
RB 3, 171, 172.

35. 10 March 1755—Order'd the Churchwardens of Wicocomoco [Wicomico] Parish for the time being bind out Elijah Ingram a Bastard child of Elizabeth Ingram according to Law. *OB 1753–56, 273.*

36. 10 March 1755—Order'd the Churchwardens of St Stephens Parish for the time being bind out Elizabeth Butterfield and Sarahann Headen Churchwell orphans according to Law. *OB 1753–56, 273.*

37. 12 May 1755—John Harding orphan of Thomas Harding deced is by the Court bound to Peter Chapman untill [until] he arrives to the age of Twenty one years. In Consideration of which the said Chapman is to Learn him the trade of a Taylor [tailor] and to Read, Write & Cypher [cipher] according to Law. Whereupon he the s^d Peter Chapman together with William Pickren his Security enter'd into Recognizance in the sum of Five thousand pounds of Tob^o for the due Performance of the same. *OB 1753–56, 312.*

38. 14 July 1755—William Hart orphan of Robert Hart deced is by the Court bound to William Swift till he arrives to the age of Twenty one years. In Consideration whereof the s^d Swift is to learn him the Trade of a Cooper and to read, write & cypher [cipher] as far as the rule of three. For the performance of which the s^d Swift with Charles Betts & John Mourison his Securities acknowledged themselves bound in the sum of 5000$^£$ of tobacco. *OB 1753–56, 346.*

39. 8 Sept. 1755—Thomas Gaskins, orphan of John Gaskins deced, is by the Court bound to John Cockrell till he arrives to the age of Twenty one years, In Consideration whereof the s^d John Cockrell is to learn him the trade of a Shoemaker and to read & write according to law, & at the Expiration of the s^d term to pay him his freedom dues. For the performance of which the s^d Cockrell together with Charles Betts & James Conway his Securities acknowledged themselves bound in the penalty of 5000$^£$ of tobacco each. *OB 1753–56, 361.*

40. 9 Sept. 1755—Order'd that the Churchwardens of Wicocomoco [Wicomico] Parish for the time being bind out Nicholas Lawless orphan of James Lawless according to Law. *OB 1753–56, 372.*

41. 13 Oct. 1755—Order'd that the Churchwardens of St Stephens Parish for the time being bind out John Cottrell orphan of Daniel Cottrell deced. according to Law. *OB 1753–56, 384.*

42. 12 Jan. 1756—Jesse Garner orphan of James Garner deced is by the Court bound to William Hadaway untill [until] he arrives to the age of Twenty one years. In Consideration of which the said Hadaway obliges himself to learn him the trade of a Taylor [tailor] & to Cypher [cipher] as far as the rule of three & at the Expiration of the s^d time to pay the s^d Garner his freedom dues. For the Performance of the same the s^d Hadaway together with Joseph Ball & William Thomas his Securities acknowledged themselves bound in the penalty of Five thousand pounds of tobacco each. *OB 1753–56, 434.*

43. 9 Feb. 1756—Order'd the Churchwardens of St Stephens Parish for the time being bind out Winnefred and Lucretia Thompson orphans of Richard

Thompson accord^g to law. *OB 1753–56, 447.*

44. 9 Feb. 1756—Order'd the Churchwardens of St Stephens Parish for the time being bind out John Talley orphan of John Talley deced. according to law. *OB 1753–56, 453.*

45. 9 Feb. 1756—Edward Barrett orphan of Nathaniel Barrett deced is by the Court bound to George Haynie for the space of four years. In consideration of which the s^d Haynie is to learn him the trade of a Joyner [joiner] and Carpenter & to read & write. For the due performance of which the s^d George Haynie together with Wm Eskridge and Thomas Brown his Securities acknowledged themselves bound in the penalty of three thousand pounds of tobacco each. *OB 1753–56, 453.*

46. 9 Feb. 1756—This Indenture Witnesseth that William Haynie Son of Sarah Haynie late of Saint Stephens Parish in the County of Northumberland as well of his own free will as by the Strict directions and appointment of the said Sarah Haynie by her last will and testament injoining [enjoining] her Exors therein named to bind the said William Haynie to the trade, art & Sciem [science] of a Joiner until he should attain to the age of Twenty one years hath put himself by the approbation of Matthew Neal one of the Exors. in the said will mentioned apprentice to George Haynie of the Parish and County aforesaid the Sciem [science] or trade which he now useth to be taught and with him after the manner of an apprentice to dwell & Serve from the date hereof untill [until] he shall attain to the age of twenty one years he being Sixteen years old the twelfth day of November last during which s^d time or term of years the s^d apprentice the said William Haynie well & truly shall serve, his secrets shall keep close, his commandments lawfull [lawful] & honest every where he shall gladly do, hurt to his said Master he shall not do nor suffer to be done in the value of one shilling or more by the year but shall let if he may or else immediately admonish his said Master then of the goods of his said Master, he shall not inordinately waste nor them to any body lend, at dice or at any other unlawful game he shall not play whereby his said Master may incult any hurt, Fornication in the house of his s^d Master or elsewhere he shall not commit, matrimony he shall not contract, Taverns he shall not frequent, with his own proper goods or any others during the said term without the Special Licence [license] of his Master, he shall not merchandize from the service of his s^d Master day or night, he shall not absent or prolong himself but in all things as good & faithful apprentice shall bear & behave himself towards his s^d Master during the time or term afores^d & the said George Haynie to his said apprentice the Science or art which he now useth Shall teach and inform or cause to be taught & informed the best way that he may or can & also Shall find to his s^d apprentice apperel [apparel] meat, drink & Bedding & all other necessarys [necessaries] neet [needed] & Convenient for an apprentice for and during the time & terms afores^d and Shall at the Expiration of his s^d time & terms of Servitude make all such other & further allowances of may & shall be by Law

required and ordered in Witness whereof the Parties to these Presents have interchangably set their hand & Seal dated the ninth day of February one thousand Seven Hundred and fifty Six and in the twenty ninth year of the Reign of our Sovereign Lord King George the Second.

Wm Haynie
George Haynie
Matthew Neale

RB 3, 269.

47. 8 March 1756—Thomas Hill orphan is by the Court bound to William Pitman untill [until] he arrives to the age of Twenty one years. In Consideration of which the s^d William Pitman is to learn him the trade of a Bricklayer & to read & write. For the due performance of which the s^d Pitman together with Robert Potts his Security acknowledged themselves bound in the penalty of three thousand pounds of tobacco. *OB 1753–56, 465.*

48. 9 March 1756—Thomas Harrison is by the Court bound to Swan Pritchard untill [until] he arrives to the age of Twenty one years. In Consideration of which the s^d Pritchard is to learn him the trade of a Weaver and to read and write. And for the due performance of which the s^d Swan Pritchard together with Charles James his security acknowledged themselves bound in the sum of three thousand pounds of tob^o. *OB 1753–56, 476.*

49. 10 May 1756—Order'd the Churchwardens of St Stephens Parish for the time being bind out Mary, Sarah, George, Charles, and Robert Christy according to Law. *OB 1756–58, 3.*

50. 10 May 1756—[page worn] Webb orphan of Moses Webb deced is by the Court bound to Joshua Palmer untill [until] he arrives to the age of twenty one years. In Consideration of wch Joshua Palmer is to learn him the trade of a Bricklayer & to read & write For the due performance thereof the said Joshua together with Swan Pritchard [page worn] acknowledged themselves bound in the sum of Five thousand pounds of tobacco. *OB 1756–58, 7.*

51. 14 June 1756—Order'd the Churchwardens of St Stephens Parish for the time being bind out Elizabeth Pugh Daughter of Thomas Pugh to Jane Hadwell & Jno Taylor according to Law. *OB 1756–58, 20.*

52. 13 Dec. 1756—Ezekiel Cotfield orphan of John Cotfield deced is by the Court bound to Dennis Swanson till he arrives to the age of Twenty one years. In Consideration of which the s^d Dennis Swanson is to learn him the trade of a Cooper and to read & write according to law. For the due performance of which the said Dennis together with William Angell his security acknowledged themselves bound in the sum of 5000$^£$ of Tobacco. *OB 1756–58, 90.*

53. 10 Jan. 1757—Henry Hurst orphan of John Hurst deced is by the Court bound to Robert Balvard till he arrives to the age of Twenty one years. In Consideration of which s^d service the s^d Robt Balvard is to learn him the Trade of a Taylor [tailor] & to read & write according to law. For the due performance of which the s^d Robert together with Saml Blackwell gen^t his Security acknowledged themselves bound in the Penalty of 5000$^£$ of tobacco. *OB 1756–58, 105.*

54. 14 Feb. 1757—George Rogers Orphan of Edward Rogers deced is by the Court bound to Stephen Chilton till he arrives to the age of twenty one years. In Consideration of which the said Stephen is to learn him the trade of a Joyner [joiner] & Carpenter and to read & write. For the performance of which the said Chilton with Joseph Wildey his security acknowledged themselves bound in the sum of 5000$^£$ of tobacco. *OB 1756–58, 119.*

55. 14 March 1757—John Pendergrass appeared in Court and agreed to serve John Wilkins the space of four years. In Consideration of which the said Wilkins is to learn him the trade of a Carpenter and to find him sufficient Clothing. *OB 1756–58, 124.*

56. 14 March 1757—John Cotrell orphan of Daniel Cotrell deced is by the Court bound to Stephen Chilton till he arrives to the age of Twenty one years. In Consideration of which the s^d Stephen is to learn him the trade of a Joyner [joiner] & Carpenter and to give him half a years Schooling. For the due Performance of which the said Stephen Chilton with William Greenwood his security acknowledged themselves bound in the penalty of 5000$^£$ of tobacco. *OB 1756–58, 125.*

57. 12 April 1757—Order'd the Churchwardens of Wicocomoco [Wicomico] Parish for the time being bind out John Mayden a Bastard child of Tabytha Mayden according to Law. *OB 1756–58, 143.*

58. 13 June 1757—George Smither orphan of George Smither deced is by the Court bound to John Yapp untill [until] he arrives to the age of Twenty one years. In Consideration thereof the said John Yapp is to learn him the trade of a Taylor [tailor]. For the due performance of which the s^d Yapp together with James Daughity and William Tosset his securities acknowledged themselves bound in the penalty of Ten thousand pounds of Tobacco. *OB 1756–58, 166.*

59. 11 July 1757—Randolph Mott orphan of Randolph Mott deced. is by the Court bound to John Yapp till he arrives to the age of twenty one years. In consideration of which the said Yapp is to learn him the trade of a Taylor [tailor]. For the due performance of which the s^d Yapp together with Elisha Betts and William Wildey his securities acknowledged themselves bound in the sum of 5000 pounds tob^o. *OB 1756–58, 172.*

60. 14 Nov. 1757—Thomas Wright son of Winfield Wright is by the Court bound to George Astin untill [until] he arrives to the age of Twenty one years.

In Consideration of which the said Astin is to learn him the trade of a Bricklayer. For the due performance of which the s^d George Astin with Winfield Wright and William Thomas his Securities acknowledg'd themselves bound in the Penalty of 5000 pounds of tobacco. *OB 1756–58, 240.*

61. 15 Nov. 1757—Ordered the Churchwardens of Wicocomoco [Wicomico] Parish bind out Chloe Swanson orphan of John Swanson deced according to law. *OB 1756–58, 245.*

62. 12 Dec. 1757—Order'd the Churchwardens of St Stephens Parish for the time being bind Baptist Gordan to John Efford according to law. *OB 1756–58, 253.*

63. 13 Feb. 1758—Peter Hack Conway orphan of George Conway deced. with his consent is by the Court bound to George McCall merch^t untill [until] Christmas 1761. On consideration of which the said McCall is to teach and instruct him in the art of merchandising and Provide for his cloathing [clothing], diet, lodging, etc. sufficient for any person in his station. And the s^d McCall further obliges himself not to remove the said Peter Hack Conway out of this Colony without his approbation. *OB 1756–58, 260.*

64. 13 Feb. 1758—Order'd the Churchwardens of Wicocomoco [Wicomico] Parish for the time being bind out the orphans of James Fitzmorris deced according to law. *OB 1756–58, 261.*

65. 13 March 1758—Order'd the Churchwardens of St Stephens Parish for the time being bind out John Gamewell orphan of John Gamewell deced according to law. *OB 1756–58, 271.*

66. 13 March 1758—Mark Harding orphan of Thomas Harding deced is by the Court bound to Robert Balvard untill [until] he arrives to the age of Twenty one years. In Consideration of which the s^d Balvard is to learn him the trade of a Taylor [tailor] and find him sufficient cloathing [clothing], Diet etc. For the due performance of which he together with Benjamin Ingram his Security acknowledged themselves bound in the penalty of five thousand pounds of tob^o. *OB 1756–58, 272.*

67. 10 July 1758—Order'd that the Churchwardens for the time being bind out Judith Mason, Jane Mason & Alice Mason orphans of Peter Mason deced according to law. *OB 1756–58, 315.*

68. 10 July 1758—John Hill orphan of Sukil Hill deced is by the Court bound to Thomas Pullen untill [until] he arives [arrives] to the age of Twenty one years, on Consideration of which the s^d Thomas Pullen is to learn him the trade of a shoemaker & provide for him sufficient Diet, cloathing [clothing], etc. For the performance of which the s^d Thomas Pullen together with John Nutt his security acknowledged themselves bound in the sum of 5000 pounds of tobacco. *OB 1756–58, 316.*

69. 14 Aug. 1758—An Indenture of apprenticeship from William Airs to William Mott with the approbation of the Court was acknowledged by the parties & admitted to record. *OB 1756–58, 320.*

70. 14 Aug. 1758—This Indenture for an apprentice Witnesseth that I William Airs the son of William Airs of the Parrish [Parish] of Saint Stephens the County of Northumberland has put himself and by these presents doth vollentarily [voluntarily] and of his own free will and accord put himself apprentice to William Mott of the same Colony a bricklear [bricklayer] to learn his trade or mistery [mystery] and after the manner of an apprentice to serve him from the date hereof for and during the term of five years next ensuing— During all which term the said apprentice his said master faithfully shall serve, his secrets keep, his lawfull [lawful] commands every where gladly obey, he shall do no damage to his said Master nor let it be done by others without letting or giving notice thereof to his said Master, he shall not waste his said goods nor lend them unlawfully to any, he shall not commit fornication nor contract marriage during the said term, at cards & dice or any other unlawfull [unlawful] games he shall not play whereby his said master shall not be damaged with his own goods nor the goods of others, he shall not absent himself day nor night from his masters service without his leave nor haunt all [ale] houses nor taverns but in all things behave himself well as a faithfull [faithful] apprentice ought to do during the said term and the said master shall use the utmost of his endeavour to teach or cause to be taught or instructed the said apprentice in the trade or mistery [mystery] he now followeth and procure & provide for him sufficient Diet, drink, aperel [apparel], Lodging & washing, making and mending fitting for an apprentice during the said term & the due performance of all & every greements [agreements] Covenants & what the Law directs for freedom Dues etc. to each parties doth bind themselves unto each other by these presents of what is above written as Witness our hands & seals we have interchangeable agreed this being the 24th day of July in the year of our Lord 1758.

          his
William W   Airs
         Mark
    William Mott

At a Court held for Northumberland County the 14th day of August 1758. This Indenture of apprenticeship between William Airs & William Mott was ackd [acknowledged] by the Parties and on the motion of the said Mott is admitted to record.

    Teste
    Thos Jones Clerk Court

RB 4, 265.

71. 14 Aug. 1758—John Murphey orphan of William Murphey deced. is by the Court bound to Griffith Williams untill [until] he arrives to the age of twenty one, he being nine years old last March. On consideration of which the s^d Griffith Williams is to learn him the trade of a weaver & provide for the s^d orphan sufficient diet, cloathing [clothing], etc. For the due performance of which the s^d Griffith together with William Thomas and James Lamkin his securities acknowledged themselves bound in the Penalty of Five thousand pounds of tobacco. *OB 1756–58, 322.*

72. 14 Aug. 1758—Thomas Robinson orphan of Thomas Robinson deced. who was formerly bound to John Foushee gent. to learn the trade of a shoemaker, personally appeared in Court & by his own consent & with the approbation of the s^d Court he is now bound to John Heath untill [until] he arrives to the age of Twenty one years. On consideration of which the said Heath is to learn him the art of a sailor & provide for him sufficient cloathing [clothing] etc. For the due performance of which the s^d John Heath together with Thomas Yerby his security acknowledged themselves bound in the penalty of Five thousand pounds of tob^o Whereupon it is order'd that the s^d John Foushee be discharged from the obligation to the s^d Robinson as aforesaid. *OB 1756–58, 323.*

73. 11 Sept. 1758—John Flynt orphan of John Flynt deced is by the Court bound to John Yapp untill [until] he arrives to the age of Twenty one years. In Consideration of which the s^d Yapp is to learn him the trade of a Taylor [tailor] & keep the s^d orphan to his learning. For the due performance of which the s^d John Yapp together with John Hobson and John Corbell his securities acknowledged themselves bound in the penalty of 5000$^£$ tobacco. *OB 1756–58, 335.*

74. 11 Sept. 1758—Cornelius Todd orphan of Cornelius Todd deced is by the Court bound to John McGoon untill [until] he arrives to the age of Twenty one years. In Consideration of which the s^d McGoon is to learn him the trade of a Weaver & to read the Bible etc. For the due performance of which the s^d McGoon together with William Taite and Samuel Eskridge his securities acknowledged themselves bound in the penalty of 5000 pounds tobacco. *OB 1756–58, 341.*

75. 11 Dec. 1758—Will of William Kenner . . . I give and commit the tuition and custody of my said son John William Hicks Kenner to my ever honoured and respected good friend, Mrs Sarah Hicks of Whitehaven aforesaid widow dureing [during] his minority not doubting but as she has hitherto she will continue to accept and execute that trust and I do recommend it to my said son that he behave himself with the greatest respect and Duty towards her and that she would Please to continue him at some school in England until he shall be fit to be bound apprentice to some business or imploym^t [employment]. . . . *RB 6, 139.*

76. 24 Dec. 1758—Will of James Blincoe . . . Item my just debts & funeral expences [expenses] being first paid, It is my will and desire that my several children which I now have by my loving wife Ann Blincoe may be & remain on my plantation & land where I now live until the youngest be able to go to trade or provide for themselves. . . . *RB 5, 106.*

77. 8 Jan. 1759—Ordered that the Churchwardens of St Stephens Parish bind out George Tillery & Thomas Tillery orphans of George Tillery dec^d and Wm Wood orphan of John Wood deced according to Law. *OB 1758–62, 10.*

78. 8 Jan. 1759—Upon the motion of Robert Belvard for discharging his apprentice Henry Hurst from further service with the Consent of Walter James his guardian. It is ordered that he be Discharged accordingly. *OB 1758–62, 10.*

79. 8 Jan. 1759—Order'd the Church^w [churchwardens] of St Stephens Parish bind out James Fontain Wilkins orphan of Thos Wilkins deced according to Law. *OB 1758–62, 11.*

80. 13 Feb. 1759—Jemima Tycer orphan of Richard Tycer deced is by the Court bound to Saml Hughlett till she arives [arrives] of Lawful age the said Hughlett is to keep her to some suitable trade & Employm^t & provide for her according to law and at the Expiration of her said time pay her freedom dues according to law for the performance of which he together with Richd Walker & John Heath bind themselves to the Justices now Sitting in 5000$^£$ Tobacco. *OB 1758–62, 18.*

81. 13 Feb. 1759—Ordered the Churchwardens of St Stephens Parish bind out Agatha Armstrong daughter of John Armstrong according to law. *OB 1758–62, 18.*

82. 9 April 1759—John Cooke Orphan of William Cooke deced is by the Court bound to John Lock till he arives [arrives] to the age of Twenty one years. The s^d Lock is to Learn him the trade of a Taylor [tailor], to read, write etc. according to Law & at the Expiration of the time aforesaid pay him his freedom dues for the performance of which the said Lock together with Kemp Hurst and George Ingram his Securitys [securities] acknowledged themselves indebted to the above Justices in 5000$^£$ of Tobacco. *OB 1758–62, 48.*

83. 14 May 1759—George Edwards Orphan of John Edwards deced is by the Court bound to Isaac Edwards till he arives [arrives] to the age of Twenty one years. The said Isaac Edwards is to learn him the trade of a cooper, to read, write and Cypher [cipher] and at the Expiration of his time to pay him freedom dues according to Law; for the performance of which the said Isaac Edwards together with Johnathan Edwards & Richard Langsdall acknowledge themselves bound to the s^d Justices now sitting their heirs and successors in 5000$^£$ of Tob^o. *OB 1758–62, 60.*

84. 9 July 1759—Wm Leach orphan of John Leach deced. is by the Court bound to Richard Watts till he arrives to the age of twenty one years to learn the trade of a Taylor [tailor], to read, write, etc. according to law; for the due performance of which Stephen Chilton & John Corbell Junr acknowledge themselves bound to the Court & their successors in the sum of 5000£ Tob^o. *OB 1758–62, 80.*

85. 14 Aug. 1759—John Gaskins orphan of John Gaskins deced is by the Court bound to Robert Davis till he arrives to the age of Twenty one years to learn the trade of a house Carpenter, to read, write etc. according to law; for the performance of which the said Davis together with James Daughity his security acknowledged themselves bound to the Court now sitting and their successors in 5,000£ of Tobacco. *OB 1758–62, 94.*

86. 1 Dec. 1759—Will of John Williams . . . I order all my sons to be bound out to some trade as soon as they have been at school and have learned arithmetick [arithmetic], reading, and writing. . . . *RB 5, 196.*

87. 10 Dec. 1759—Ordered the Churchwardens of St Stephens Parish bind out William, Peter, Catherine, and John Wilkins orphans of Thomas Wilkins deced according to law. *OB 1758–62, 125.*

88. 10 Dec. 1759—John Lunsford is by the Court bound to William Campbell till he arrives to the age of twenty one years; in consideration whereof the said Campbell is to learn him the trade of a joiner & Turner, to read, write, etc. according to law and at the expiration of his said time to pay him freedom dues for the performance of which the said Campbell together with Hugh Watson his security acknowledged themselves, their heirs, etc. bound to Spencer Ball, Samuel Blackwell, John Foushee & William Taite gent. Justices now sitting in the sum of 5,000£ Tobacco. *OB 1758–62, 128.*

89. 23 Jan. 1760—Will of Joseph Hague . . . Likewise it is my desire that my son Francis Hague be bound out to a Taylor [tailor] & my daughter Hannah Hague bound out to learn to be a weaver. . . . *RB 5, 197.*

90. 10 March 1760—John Hill Orphan of John Hill deced is by the Court bound to Peter Bean till he arives [arrives] to the age of Twenty one years to learn the trade of a Taylor [tailor], to read, write etc. according to law & at the Expiration of his time to pay him freedom dues. For the performance of which the said Bean together with Charles Copedge his security acknowledged themselves Indebted to the Court now sitting & their successors in 5,000£ of Tobacco. *OB 1758–62, 153.*

91. 10 March 1760—John Hill Orphan of Luke Hill deced is by the Court bound to Henry Barns till he arives [arrives] to the age of Twenty one years to learn the trade of a shoemaker, to read, write etc. according to law & at the expiration of his time to pay him freedom dues. For the performance of which the s^d Barnes together with Robert Clarke his Security acknowledges themselves indebted to the Court now sitting and their successors in 5,000$^£$ tob^o. *OB 1758–62, 153.*

92. 14 April 1760—James Sutton Orphan of William Sutton deced is by the Court Bound to Robert Belvard till he arives [arrives] to the age of Twenty one years to learn the trade of a Taylor [tailor], to read, write, and Cypher [cipher] according to Law and at the Expiration of his time to pay him his freedom dues for the performance of which the said Belvard together with Moses Lunsford his security acknowledged themselves bound to the Court now sitting and their successors in the sum of 5000$^£$ of Tobacco. *OB 1758–62, 171.*

93. 14 April 1760—James Barns orphan of Edward Barns deced. is by the Court bound to Thomas Brown (to learn the trade of a cooper, to read, write, etc. according to law) till he arrives to the age of twenty one years and the said Brown is to pay him his freedom dues for the performance of which the said Brown together with Samuel Eskridge his security acknowledge themselves bound to the Court now sitting & their successors in the sum of 5,000$^£$ of Tobacco. *OB 1758–62, 173.*

94. 12 May 1760—Ezekiel Coffee orphan of James Coffee is by the Court bound to Charles James till he arives [arrives] to the age of twenty one years; the said James is to learn him to read & write etc. according to law and to pay him his freedom dues for the performance of which the said Charles James together with Wm Angel his Security acknowledged themselves bound to the Court now sitting, their heirs and successors in 5,000$^£$ of Tobacco. *OB 1758–62, 179.*

95. 27 Jan. 1761—Will of Cornelious Sullivan ... Item my will is that my son Dennis should be bound to learn the Trade of a Taylor [tailor]. Item my will is that my son Cornelious also be bound to learn the trade of a Taylor [tailor] also that both my other sons Jesse and Thomas be bound to learn the trade of a Taylor [tailor]. Item my will is that both my daughters Chloe and Nancy shall be bound to learn the trade of a weaver. Item my will is that my four sons be learn'd [learned] to read & write & Cypher [cipher] thro the rule of three. Item my will is that my two daughters be learn'd [learned] to read.... *RB 5, 304.*

96. 9 Feb. 1761—John Harding Orphan of Thomas Harding deced is by the Court Bound to Thomas Blincoe untill [until] he arives [arrives] to the age of twenty one years according to Law. The said Blincoe is to learn him the trade of a house Carpenter; for the performance of which the said Thomas Blincoe together with John Cralle Junr & John Blincoe his securities acknowledge themselves indebted to the Court now sitting & their successors in 5000$^£$ of tob^o. *OB 1758–62, 241.*

97. 9 Feb. 1761—John Mott orphan of Mosley Mott deced is by the Court Bound to William Mott for the time of three years the said Wm Mott is to learn him the trade of a Bricklayer for the performance of which the said Wm Mott together with Elisha Betts acknowledges themselves bound to the Court now sitting and their successors in 5,000£ of tobacco. *OB 1758–62, 244.*

98. 9 Feb. 1761—Edwin Lunsford Orphan of Swanson Lunsford deced is by the Court bound to Peter Bean untill [until] he arives [arrives] to the age of twenty one years to learn the trade of a Taylor [tailor], to read, write & Cypher [cipher] to the rule of three; for the performance of which the said Bean together with Charles James and Isaac Lunsford his securities acknowledge themselves bound to the Court now sitting and their successors in the sum of 5000£ of tobacco. *OB 1758–62, 245.*

99. 9 Feb. 1761—Order'd the Churchwardens of Saint Stephens Parish bind out Betty and Sally Ashburn orphans of William Ashburn deced, Peter Wilkins orphan of Thomas Wilkins and George Curtice orphan of John Curtice deced according to Law. *OB 1758–62, 246.*

100. 9 Feb. 1761—Order'd the Churchwardens of Wiccocomoco [Wicomico] Parish bind out Alice Warrick orphan of Richard Warrick deced according to Law. *OB 1758–62, 246.*

101. 9 Feb. 1761—Order'd the Churchwardens of St Stephens Parish bind out John Davis and Eliz^a Davis orphans of John Davis deced according to Law. *OB 1758–62, 246.*

102. 9 Feb. 1761—Robuck Hudson Orphan of Rodham Hudson deced is by the Court bound to George Haynie till he arives [arrives] to the age of twenty one years; the said Haynie is to Learn him the trade of a house carpenter and Joiner; for the performance of which the said Haynie together with Thomas Brown & Henry Boggess his Securities acknowledge themselves bound to the Court now sitting and their successors in 5000£ of tobacco. *OB 1758–62, 246.*

103. 10 Feb. 1761—Thomas Vibratt orphan of Lancelot Vibratt deced is by the Court bound to Benjamin Vanlandingham Junr till he arives [arrives] to the age of twenty one years the said Vanlandingham to learn him the trade of a shoemaker & to read, write & Cypher [cipher] to the rule of three according to Law for the Performance of which the said Vanlandingham together with George Vanlandingham his Security acknowlesdges themselves bound to the Court now setting [sitting] & their successors in 5000£ tob^o. *OB 1758–62, 254.*

104. 13 April 1761—This Indenture made this 13th day of April in the year of our Lord 1761 Witnesseth that Richard Corbell a bastard Child of Judith Blundell hath of his own free & Voluntary will (or by & with the Consent of his

Mother) placed & bound himself apprentice unto George Phillips of the County of North^d & Parish of Wiccocomoco [Wicomico] Mill Wright to be Taught in the said Trade, Science, or Occupation of a Mill Wright which he the said George Phillips now useth & with him as an apprentice to dwell Continue and Serve from the day of the date hereof untill [until] he the said Richard Corbell shall arive [arrive] or attain to the age of Twenty three years during all which said Term the said Apprentice his said Master will & faithfully shall serve, his secrets keep, his lawfull command everywhere gladly do, Hurt to his said Master he shall not do nor willfully suffer to be done but the same to his power shall let or forth will give notice thereof to his said Master, the goods of his said Master he shall not imbezzle [embezzle] or waste nor lend them without his Consent to any, at Cards, dice or any other unlawfull games he shall not play, Taverns or ale houses he shall not haunt or frequent, Fornication he shall not commit, Matrimony he shall not contract, from the service of his said Master he shall not at any time depart or absent himself without his said Masters leave but in all things as a good & faithfull Apprentice shall & well Demean & behave himself toward his said Master & all his during the said Term and the said Master his said Apprentice the said Trade, Science or occupation of a mill wright which he now useth will all things thereunto belonging shall & will Teach & Instruct or otherwise Cause to be well & sufficiently Taught & Instructed after the best way & manner that he can & also the said George Phillips will Cause or Procure that the said Apprentice shall be Taught to read, Write & Cypher [cipher] as far as the rule of three and shall & will also find & allow his said Apprentice Meat, Drink, Washing, Lodging & Apparel [apparel] both Linen & woolen and all other necessaries both in sickness & in health meet and Convenient for such an apprentice during the Term afores^d and at the end of the said Term shall & will give to his said apprentice (over and above his then Cloathing [clothing]) one new suit of apperrel [apparel] (viz: Coat Waistcoat breeches Hatt shoes and stockings with suitable linen as is fit & usual for such an apprentice) In Witness whereof the said Parties to these Presents have Interchangeably set their hand & affixed their Seals the day & year first above written.   his

                   Richard   Corbell
                       mark
                   George Phillips

RB 5, 392, 393.

105.   13 April 1761—Joseph Davis Orphan of John Davis deced is by the Court bound to John Lancaster till he arrives to the age of Twenty one years the said Lancasters to learn him the Trade of a shoe maker, to read, Write & Cypher [cipher] according to Law for the performance of which the said John Lancaster together with Richard Claughton Junr his security acknowledges themselves Bound to the Court now Setting [sitting] and to their successors 5,000$^£$ of tobacco. *OB 1758–62, 265.*

106. 13 April 1761—Joseph Bridgman orphan of Joseph Bridgman deced is by the Court bound to Stephen Chilton till he arrives to the age of Twenty one years, the said Chilton to learn him the trade of a Joyner [joiner] and to read, write & Cypher [cipher] according to Law for the due performance of which the said Chilton together with John Corbell his security acknowledges themselves bound to the Court now setting [sitting] & their successors in 5000$^£$ of Tobacco. *OB 1758–62, 266.*

107. 10 Aug. 1761—An Indenture of apprenticeship between Andrew Anderson & Fielding Bennet was acknowledged by the said Anderson and Bennet & ordered to be recorded. *OB 1758–62, 313.*

108. 10 Aug. 1761—This Indenture Witnesseth that it is agreed and fully ended betwixt Andrew Anderson of Northumberland County and Parish of St Stephens Chair Maker and painter of the one part and Fielding Bennett Son of Robert Bennett Deced of the same Parish and County of the other part as followeth that the said Fielding Bennett hereby binds himself an apprentice to the aforesaid Andrew Anderson to learn the trade and mistery [mystery] of a Chair Maker and painter and that for the space of three years from and after the Date of these presents which is hereby declared to be his entry to his said apprenticeship during which time the said Fielding Bennett binds and obliges himself that he shall faithfully and honestly serve his said master in the station and duty aforesaid and that by night and by Day no Day excepted shall not absent himself there from without liberty asked and obtained otherway to serve two Days for each Days absence after the expiration of this Indenture otherways he shall forfit [forfeit] the Penalty herein after mentioned and make payment thereof to the said Andrew Anderson and that he shall not reveal his said Masters secrets nor conceal any thing that may tend to the hurt or prejudice of his said Master but discover the same so as it may be prevented, that he shall not frequent or keep Idle company or debotched [debauched] Company nor play at Cards, dice, fives or any other game whereby he may neglect his said Masters Service, he shall not frequent publick [public] houses, tipling houses or any where liquor is sold and for the more sure and dutiful performance of the premises the said Fielding Bennett hereby binds himself to pay or cause to be paid to his said Master fifty pounds if he fails to perform all and every part of the above contract.

For the which causes and on the other part the said Andrew Anderson Binds and obliges himself to learn and instruct so far as he is able and the said Bennett is capable of taking during the said term the Trade of a Chair maker and Painter and shall maintain and entertain him in board, washing, mending and making and sufficient cloaths [clothes] and at the Expiration of the time to give him a sute [suit] of good cloaths [clothes], also three pounds ten shillings cash to the performance of the above, the said Andrew Anderson binds himself in the sum of fifty pounds if he fails in the performance of his part of the above in

Witness whereof both parties have subscribed this present Indenture and affixed their seals this tenth Day of August in the year of our Lord 1761.

            A. Anderson
            Fielding Bennet
RB 5, 451, 452.

109. 14 Sept. 1761—Walter Jones orphan of Solomon Jones is by the Court bound to Richard Thomson until he arrives to the age of Twenty one years, the said Thomson to learn him the Trade of a Ship Joiner and to read, write and cipher as far as the rule of three; for the performance of which he together with William Eskridge and Henry Boggess his securities acknowledge themselves indebted to the Justices now sitting and their successors in 5000£ of Tobacco. *OB 1758–62, 321.*

110. 14 Sept. 1761—Upon the motion of Church Wardens of Wiccomoco [Wicomico] Parrish [Parish] it is ordered they bind out Richard Porter Dammeron, William Dammeron, John and James Dammeron Orphans of William Dammeron Junr Deced according to Law. *OB 1758–62, 322.*

111. 15 Sept. 1761—It is ordered the Churchwardens of Wiccocomoco [Wicomico] Parish Bind out Ellis & Thomas Gill orphans of Thomas Gill Deceased according to Law & also that they Bind out Sarah and Margaret Dammeron children of Moses Dammeron. *OB 1758–62, 324.*

112. 12 Oct. 1761—Dennis Sullivan orphan of Cornelius Sullivan Deceased aged fifteen years next Christmas is bound to Charles Carter until he is twenty one years of age; according to Law the said Carter [is] to learn him the Trade of a carpenter for the performance of which the said Carter together with William Blackerby his security acknowledged themselves indebted Five Thousand Pounds of Tob^o to the Justices now sitting and to their successors. *OB 1758–62, 333.*

113. 8 Feb. 1762—Richard and William Rowt Orphans of John Rowt Deceased and with the consent of William Taite their guardian agreed to be Bound to John Efferd untill [until] they arrive to the age of Twenty one years, the said Efferd to Learn them the trade of a House Carpenter and Mill Wright for the performance of which the said Efferd together with John Rowt, and Antony Rowt his securitys [securities] acknowledged themselves Indebted to the Justices now sitting in the sum of Ten thousand Pounds of Tobacco. *OB 1758–62, 351.*

114. 9 Feb. 1762—William Betts Orphan of Charles Betts Deceased is by the Court Bound to William Mott untill [until] he arrives to the age of Twenty one years according to Law the said Mott to Learn him the Trade of a Brick layer etc. for the performance of which the said Mott together with Elisha Betts his

Security acknowledges themselves Bound to the Court now Sitting in the sum of Five Thousand Pounds of Tobacco. *OB 1758–62, 352.*

115. 9 Feb. 1762—John Betts Orphan of Charles Betts Deceased, Spencer Nelms Orphan of Aaron Nelms Deceased, Josias Gaskins Orphan of Josias Gaskins Deceased, Norman Appleby Orphan of John Appleby Deceased is by the Court bound to James Templeman till they arrive to the age of Twenty one years according to Law. The said Templeman to learn them the Trade of a Taylor [tailor]; whereupon the said James Templeman together with Joseph Ball and George Smither his Securities acknowledge themselves Bound to the Court now Sitting in the sum of Five thousand Pounds of tobacco each. *OB 1758–62, 353.*

116. 9 Feb. 1762—James Fountain Wilkins orphan of Thomas Wilkins Deceased is by the Court bound to John Morriss according to Law until he arrives to the age of Twenty one years, the said Morriss to learn him the Trade of a shoemaker for the performance of which the said Morriss together with John Christopher and Jesse Alexander his securities acknowledge themselves Bound to the Court now sitting in the sum of Five Thousand Pounds of Tobacco. *OB 1758–62, 354.*

117. 9 Feb. 1762—William Collins Orphan of Timothy Collins Deceased is by the Court Bound to George Smither according to Law untill [until] he arrives to the age of Twenty one years the said Smither to learn him the Trade of a Taylor [tailor] etc Whereupon the said Smither together with James Templeman and Randolph Mott his Securities acknowledged themselves Bound to the Court now Sitting in the Sum of Five Thousand Pounds of Tob^o. *OB 1758–62, 354.*

118. 9 Feb. 1762—Daniel James Orphan of Thomas James Deceased is by the Court Bound to Charles Barrott according to Law untill [until] he arrives to the age of Twenty one years the said Barrott to Learn him the Trade of a Shoemaker and to Read, Write etc for the Performance of which the said Barrott together with Onesephorus Harvey his Security acknowledges themselves Bound to the Court now sitting in the sum of Five Thousand Pounds of Tobacco. *OB 1758–62, 354.*

119. 9 Feb. 1762—Isaac Kirk Orphan of George Kirk Deceased is by the Court Bound to Hopkins Harding according to Law untill [until] he arrives to the age of Twenty one years the said Harding to Learn him the Trade of a Bricklayer for the Performance of which the said Harding together with John Knight his Security acknowledges themselves Bound to the Court now sitting in the sum of Five Thousand Pounds of Tobacco. *OB 1758–62, 355.*

120. 9 Feb. 1762—William Webb Orphan of William Webb Deceased is by the

Court Bound to Charles Coppedge Junr untill [until] he arrives to the age of Twenty one years according to Law the said Coppedge to learn him the Trade of a Taylor [tailor] and to Read, Write etc for the performance of which the said Charles Coppedge together with William Coppedge his security acknowledges themselves Bound to the Court now sitting in the sum of Five Thousand Pounds of Tobacco. *OB 1758–62, 355.*

121. 9 Feb. 1762—Aaron Nelms Son of Aaron Nelms Deceased is by the Court Bound to Hopkins Harding to serve till he is Twenty one years of age according to Law. The said Harding to Learn him the Trade of a Bricklayer for the Performance of which the said Harding together with John Knight his Security acknowledges themselves Bound to the Court now sitting in the sum of Five Thousand Pounds of Tobacco. *OB 1758–62, 358.*

122. 8 March 1762—An Indenture of an apprenticeship between Joshua Harper and Thomas Colston acknowledged and Ordered to be Recorded. *OB 1758–62, 360.*

123. 8 March 1762—This Indenture made this Twenty Third Day of February in the year of our Lord one Thousand Seven Hundred and Sixty two Witnesseth that I Joshua Harper of the Parish of St Stephens in the County of North^d of my own free will have put an [and] Placed and by these Presents do put and place my son James Harper an apprentice to Thomas Colston of the Parish of Coply in the County of Westmoreland with him to dwell and to serve from the Date of these Presents untill [until] the said James Harper shall arive [arrive] to the age of Twenty one years; during all which Term the said apprentice his said Master faithfully to Serve according to his Power and Ability and Honestly and Obediently in all Things demean himself towards his said Master during the said Term and the said Thomas Colston his Heirs Exors etc. Doth Covenant and agree with the above said Joshua Harper his Heirs Exors and by these Presents that he the said Thomas Colston will find Provide for and Constantly allow unto the said James Harper sufficient Meat, Drink, Lodging and Apparrell [apparel] and all other Things neadfull [needful] and Necessary for such a apprentice and likewise to teach him the said James Harper the Art and Trade of a Taylor [tailor] and constantly to keep him the said James Harper at the above said Trade Teaching and Instructing him therein during the whole Term of his apprenticeship and the said Thomas Colston doth farther agree with the above—Joshua Harper that on failure of any one perticular [particular] by him the said Thomas Colston herein covenanted promised or agreed to be performed by him the said Thomas in behalf of: for or to the above said James Harper and if he dose [does] not learn him to read and write the same being proved by the oath of one or more Witness that then the above said James Harper shall by these Presents as free and freely acquited [acquitted] and discharged from the said Thomas Colston as if this Indenture had never been made. In witness whereof I have hereunto set my Hand and affix my Seal the

Day and year first above written.

Joshua his mark Harper

Thomas his mark Colston

RB 6, 556, 557.

124. 8 March 1762—Ezekiel Coffee an apprentice to Charles James applying to the Court to be discharged from his said Master it appearing to the Court he had Served his Time according to Law it is therefore ordered that he be discharged from his said Master. *OB 1758–62, 361.*

125. 12 April 1762—William Cook Orphan of William Cook deceased is by the Court bound to Robert Belvard untill [until] he arrives to the age of Twenty one years according to Law the said Belvard to learn him the Trade of a Taylor [tailor] and to Read, Write etc for the performance of which the said Robert Belvard together with John Cook his Security acknowledges themselves Bound to the Justices now Sitting and their Successors in the sum of Five thousand Pounds of Tobacco. *OB 1758–62, 367.*

126. 12 April 1762—John Burrows Orphan of Charles Burrows Deceased is by the Court Bound to Francis Rolls untill [until] he arrives to the age of Twenty one years the said Rolls to learn him the Trade of a Shoemaker and to Read, Write etc according to Law for the Performance of which the said Rolls together with Edwin [not legible] his Security acknowledges themselves Bound to the Justices now Sitting and their Successors in the Sum of Five Thousand Pounds of Tobacco. *OB 1758–62, 368.*

127. 12 April 1762—An Indenture of Apprenticeship between Isaac Mott and Randolph Mott acknowledged and ordered to be Recorded. *OB 1758–62, 368.*

128. 12 April 1762—This Indenture Witnesseth that Isaac Mott the son of Randal Mott in the County of North^d hath put himself and by these presents doth Voluntarily & of his own free will & accord put himself apprentice to Randle Mott of the same Collony [colony], a Taylor [tailor] to learn his Trade or mistery [mystery] on after the manner of an apprentice to serve him from the day of the date hereof, for or during all which term, of Four years next ensuing; during all which term the s^d apprentice his master faithfully shall serve, his secrets keep, his lawfull [lawful] commands every where gladly obey, he shall do no damage to his Master, nor see it to be done by others, without letting or giving notice thereof to his master—He shall not commit Fornication nor Contract Matrimony during the s^d Term—At cards, Dice or any other unlawful games—he shall not absent himself Day nor Night from his master's service without his leave; nor haunt ale houses, taverns or Playhouses but in all things behave himself as a Faithful apprentice ought to do, during the s^d Term, and the s^d master shall use the utmost of his endeavour to teach or cause to be taught or instructed the s^d apprentice in Trade or mistery [mystery] he now followeth, & procure & provide for him sufficient meat, Drink, Aparrel [apparel], lodging & washing fiting [fitting] for an apprentice during the s^d Term, and for the due performance of all & every the s^d covenants & agreements either of the s^d parties bind themself [themselves] unto the other by these presents, In Witness whereof we have hereunto set our hands & Seals this Twelfth Day of April, one Thousand seven hundred & sixty two.

Isaac Mott
Randle Mott

RB 6, 13.

129.   12 April 1762—Ordered the Churchwardens of Wiccocomoco [Wicomico] Parish bind out Judith Hammond Daughter of Peter Hammond according to Law. *OB 1758–62, 368.*

130.   14 Sept. 1762—Order'd the Churchwardens of St Stephens Parish for the time being bind out Robert Waters according to law. *OB 1758–62, 522.*

131.   14 Sept. 1762—Order'd that the Churchwardens of St Stephens Parish for the time being bind out Letty Trop Orphan of Moses Trop deced according to Law. *OB 1758–62, 522.*

132.   11 Oct. 1762—John Elmore orphan of Josiah Elmore deced is by the Court bound to Richd Thompson untill [until] he arrives to the age of Twenty one years, he being fourteen years old or thereabouts, on Consideration of which the s^d Thompson is to learn him the trade of a Joiner & to provide for him according to Law. For the Performance of which the s^d Thompson with Peter Lamkin & Thomas Brown his securities acknowledges themselves their Heirs etc Indebted to the Justices now setting & their successors in the sum of 5000$^£$ tob^o. *OB 1758–62, 538.*

133.   11 Oct. 1762—Order'd that the Churchwardens of St Stephens Parish for the time being bind out Elizabeth Hayden daughter of Lewis Hayden according to law. *OB 1758–62, 540.*

134.   9 Nov. 1762—John Palmer orphan of James Palmer deced is by the Court bound to John Wilkins untill [until] he arrives to full age. On Consideration of which the s^d Wilkins is to learn him the trade of a shoemaker & to provide for the s^d Palmer during the s^d Term all necessaries according to Law. For the performance of which the s^d Jno Wilkins wth Joseph Ball his security acknowledged themselves bound to the Court now setting in the sum of 5000$^£$ tob^o each. *OB 1762–66, Part 1, 13.*

135. 13 Dec. 1762—John Cornish orphan of Richard Cornish deced being sixteen years old next February is by the Court bound to John Kirk untill [until] he arrives to the age of Twenty one years. On Consideration of which the s^d Kirk is to learn him the trade of a Carpenter and Joyner [joiner] & to provide him all other necessaries according to Law. For the Performance of which the s^d John Kirk together with wth Kemp Hurst his security acknowledged themselves bound to the Justices now setting [sitting] & their successors in the sum of 5000$^£$ tobo. *OB 1762–66, Part 1, 19.*

136. 13 Dec. 1762—Christopher Mayes orphan of John Mayes deced being sixteen years old next June is by the Court bound to Richard Greenstreet untill [until] he arrives to the age of Twenty one years. On Consideration of which the s^d Greenstreet is to learn him the trade of a Carpenter & to provide for him all other necessaries according to law. For the Performance of which the s^d Richard together with John Greenstreet his security acknowledged themselves bound to the Justices now setting [sitting] & their successors in the sum of 5000$^£$ tobo. *OB 1762–66, Part 1, 19.*

137. 10 Jan. 1763—Order'd that the Churchwardens of St Stephens Parish for the time being bind out Mary Parker orphan of Thomas Parker deced to Richard Claughton Junr according to law. *OB 1762–66, Part 1, 30.*

138. 10 Jan. 1763—Order'd that the Churchwardens of St Stephens Parish for the time being bind out John Summers orphan of William Summers deced to Richard Claughton Junr according to law. *OB 1762–66, Part 1, 31.*

139. 10 Jan. 1763—Ord'd that the Churchwardens of St Stephens Parish for the time being bind out Nancy Trap orphan of Moses Trap according to law. *OB 1762–66, Part 1, 31.*

140. 14 Feb. 1763—Order'd that the Churchwardens of St Stephens Parish for the time being bind out Sarah Kesterson Daughter of William Kesterson deced. according to law. *OB 1762–66, Part 1, 34.*

141. 14 Feb. 1763—John Tounsend being eleven years old is by the Court bound to Francis Yeates untill [until] he arrives to the age of Twenty one years. On Consideration of which the said Yeates is to learn him the trade of a Taylor [tailor] & to provide for him such necessaries as by law is required. For the due performance of which the s^d Francis Yeates together with William Bailey his security acknowledged themselves Indebted to the Justices now sitting in the sum of 5000$^£$ tob^a. [The index reads Townsend, not Tounsend.] *OB 1762–66, Part 1, 36.*

142. 14 Feb. 1763—Upon the Petition of Mary Walker against Francis Roles for ill usuage [usage] to her son. It is ordered that unless the s^d Roles give better usuage [usage] to the s^d Orphan that he be discharged from the service. *OB 1762–66, Part 1, 36.*

143. 14 March 1763—Fielding Coward son of William Coward being seventeen years old in April next is by the Court bound to Allen Long Shiverill untill [until] he arrives to the age of Twenty one years. On Consideration of which the said Shiverill is to learn him to Read, Write & Cypher [cipher] as also to teach & Instruct him in the Art & Trade of a ship carpenter & to provide for him such necessaries as by law is required. For the due Performance of which the said Shiverell together with Griffin Fauntleroy and John Douglas his securities acknowledged themselves Indebted to the Justices now sitting in the Penalty of 5000[£] tob^o. *OB 1762–66, Part 1, 39.*

144. 14 March 1763—John Nutt orphan of Farnefold Nutt is by the Court bound to John Nutt untill [until] he arrives to the age of Twenty one years. On Consideration of which the said Jno Nutt is to learn him the trade of a Carpenter & to provide for him such necessaries as by law is required. For the due performance of which the s^d John Nutt together with Joseph Nutt and John Knight his securities acknowledged themselves Indebted to the Justices now sitting in the sum of 5000[£] tob^o. *OB 1762–66, Part 1, 40.*

145. 9 May 1763—Orderd that the Churchwardens of Wicocomoco [Wicomico] Parish for the time being bind out Nicholas Lawler son of James Lawler according to Law. *OB 1762–66, Part 1, 99.*

146. 16 June 1763—Haynie Townsend son of William Townsend is by the Court bound to William Mott (with the consent of the s^d William Townsend) untill [until] he arrives to the age of Twenty one years. In Consideration of which the said William Mott is to learn him the trade of a Bricklayer and to find and provide for the s^d Haynie Townsend during the said Term good and sufficient cloathing [clothing], meat, drink, washing and Lodging. For the due Performance of which the said William Mott together with Ewell Alexander his Security acknowledged themselves bound to the Court now setting in the sum of Five thousand pounds of Tobacco. *OB 1762–66, Part 1, 159.*

147. 11 July 1763—On the Petition of Mary Walker against Francis Roles for ill usage to her son John Burros, on hearing the witness of each party and this being the second complaint, It is order'd that the s^d John Burros be Discharged from the s^d Roles. *OB 1762–66, Part 1, 170.*

148. 11 July 1763—Ordered that the Churchwardens of St Stephens Parish for the time being bind out John Burros an Orphan according to law. *OB 1762–66, Part 1, 170.*

149. 8 Aug. 1763—William Danks orphan of George Danks deced is by the Court bound to William Morton untill [until] he arrives at the age of Twenty one years, he being born the 14th day of Dec' 1751 On Consideration of which the s^d Morton is to learn his s^d apprentice to read, write, and Cypher [cipher] and also the trade of a Taylor [tailor] & to find and provide for him sufficient cloathing [clothing], meat, drink, washing and lodging. For the due performance of which the said Morton with William Taite and David Boyd his securities acknowledged themselves bound to the Court in the Penalty of 5,000£ tob°. *OB 1762–66, Part 1, 189.*

150. 8 Aug. 1763—Order'd that the Churchwardens of St Stephens Parish for the time being bind out Judith Leach an orphan according to Law. *OB 1762–66, Part 1, 193.*

151. 9 Aug. 1763—Order'd the Churchwardens of St Stephens Parish for the time being bind out James, Thomas and William Johnstone's [Johnstone,] orphans of Thomas Johnstone deced according to Law. *OB, 1762–66, Part 1, 198.*

152. 12 Sept. 1763—Henry Robertson Came into Court and agreed to serve Richard Bowes for the Term of two years thence next ensuing, on Consideration of which the s^d Bowes is to teach him the Trade of a Ship Carpenter & to find & provide for the s^d Robinson during the s^d Term sufficient Diet, washing and Lodging, also the s^d Bowes is to pay the s^d Robinson the sum of Twenty pounds which s^d sum is to be paid Quarterly. For the due Performance of which the s^d Richard Bowes together with George Simpson his security acknowledged themselves bound to the Court now setting [sitting] in the sum of 5000£ tob°. *OB 1762–66, Part 1, 203.*

153. 10 Oct. 1763—Charles McCalley orphan of Charles McCalley deced is by the Court bound to John McCalley untill [until] he arrives to the age of Twenty one years. In Consideration of which the said McCalley is to learn him the Trade of a Joyner [joiner] & carpenter & also to provide for him such necessaries as is by the law required during the s^d Term. For the Performance of which the s^d John McCalley together with William Taite his security ack^d themselves Indebted to the Justices now setting [sitting] in the Penalty of 5000£ tob°. *OB 1762–66, Part 1, 224.*

154. 11 Oct. 1763—William Jones orphan of John Jones deced is by the Court bound to George Haynie untill [until] he arrives at the age of Twenty one years, On Consideration of which the s^d Haynie is to learn him the Trade of a Carpenter & Joyner [joiner] & to find & provide for his s^d apprentice during the s^d Term good & sufficient apperrel [apparel], meat, Drink, washing & lodging. For the due Performance of which the said George Haynie together with Samuel Eskridge his Security acknowledg^d themselves bound to the Justices now setting [sitting] & their successors in the Penalty of 5000£ Tobacco. *OB 1762–66, Part 1, 242.*

155. 12 Dec. 1763—Richard Garner is by the Court bound to John McCalley for the Term of six years on Consideration of which the s^d McCalley is to learn him the trade of a Carpenter & Joyner [joiner] and to find for him sufficient Apperrel [apparel], meat, drink, washing & lodging. For the due performance of which the s^d McCalley together with William Taite gent. his Security acknowledged themselves bound to the Justices now setting [sitting] & their successors in the Penalty of 5,000£ tob^o (good suit of cloths when free). *OB 1762–66, Part 1, 251.*

156. 12 Dec. 1763—Order'd that the Churchwardens of St Stephens Parish for the time being bind out Bibby, Isaac, Betty, and Susannah Bush orphans of John Bush deceased according to Law. *OB 1762–66, Part 1, 251.*

157. 9 Jan. 1764—Orderd that the Churchwardens of St Stephens Parish for the time being bind out Mary Parker orphan of Thomas Parker deced according to law. *OB 1762–66, Part 1, 262.*

158. 9 Jan. 1764—Order'd that the Churchwardens of St Stephens Parish for the time being bind out John Denny, orphan of John Denny deced according to Law. *OB 1762–66, Part 1, 264.*

159. 13 Feb. 1764—Rodham Trussell orphan of John Trussell deced is by the Court bound to Isaac Richardson untill [until] he arrives at the age of Twenty one years. On Consideration of which the s^d Isaac is to learn him the trade of a mill Right [millwright] & Carpenter & to find him sufficient cloathing [clothing], meat, drink, washing & lodging. For the due performance of which the s^d Isaac together with Samuel Eskridge and Patrick Mealey his securities acknowledged themselves bound to the Justices now sitting and their successors in the sum of 5000£ tobacco. *OB 1762–66, Part 1, 267.*

160. 13 Feb. 1764—Edwin Gaskins orphan of Josiah Gaskins is by the Court bound to Mark Harding untill [until] he arrives at the age of Twenty one years, on Consideration of which the s^d Harding is to learn him the trade of a Taylor [tailor], & find & Provide for him sufficient schooling, cloathing [clothing], meat, drink, washing & lodging for the due Performance of which the s^d Harding together with Hopkins Harding his security acknowledged themselves bound to the Justices now setting [sitting] & their successors in the sum of 5000£ tob^o. *OB 1762–66, Part 1, 269.*

161. 12 March 1764—Order'd that the Churchwardens of St Stephens Parish for the time being bind out John Brown orphan of William Brown deced according to Law. *OB 1762–66, Part 1, 273.*

162. 12 March 1764—Order'd that the Churchwardens of S^t. Stephens Parish for the time being bind out Rodham, Samuel, and Shapleigh French orphans of John French deced according to Law. *OB 1762–66, Part 1, 273.*

39

163. 12 March 1764—On the Petition of Robuck Hudson against George Haynie for his Freedom. It appears to the Court that the s^d Robuck is not free untill [until] the Expiration of thirty three days from this date. *OB 1762–66, Part 1, 273.*

164. 10 April 1764—Orderd that the Churchwardens of St Stephens Parish for the time being bind John Burros orphan of Charles Burros to Edwin Farned according to Law. *OB 1762–66, Part 1, 309.*

165. 14 May 1764—Order'd that the Churchwardens of St Stephens Parish for the time being bind out Joanne Blincoe orphan of John Blincoe deced according to Law. *OB 1762–66, Part 1, 321.*

166. 11 June 1764—Orderd that the Churchwardens of St Stephens Parish for the time being bind out Mary Hardee orphan of Parrot Hardee deced according to law. *OB 1762–66, Part 2, 349.*

167. 11 Feb. 1765—Reid Hutt orphan of Thomas Hutt deced. is by the Court bound to Richard Thompson untill [until] he arrives to the age of Twenty one years. In consideration of which the sd. Thompson is to learn him the trade of a shop Joyner [joiner], & during all which time he is to find & provide for the said Hutt good clothing and diet. For the Performance of which the said Thompson together with William Bailey his security acknowledged themselves bound to this Court in the sum of 5,000$^£$ Tobacco. *OB 1762–66, Part 2, 452.*

168. 11 March 1765—Leroy West (by his consent) is by the Court bound to John McCalley untill [until] he arrives to the age of Twenty one years. On Consideration of which the s^d McCalley is to learn him the trade of a Carpenter and Joyner [joiner], & to find him sufficient Diet, washing & lodging, and William Taite gent. agrees to find the s^d Leroy West clothing out of the estate of the s^d West he being his guardian. For the Performance on the part of the s^d McCalley he with the s^d Taite his security acknowledged themselves bound to this Court in the sum of 5000$^£$ Tobacco. *OB 1762–66, Part 2, 456.*

169. 11 March 1765—John Sebree orphan of John Sebree deced is by the Court bound to George Astin untill [until] he arrives to the age of Twenty one years. In Consideration of which the s^d Astin is to learn him the trade of a Bricklayer and to find & provide for him sufficient clothing, meat, Drink, washing and lodging. For the due Performance of which the s^d George Astin together with James Smith his security acknowledged themselves bound to the Court in the Penalty of 5000$^£$ tobo. *OB 1762–66, Part 2, 457.*

170. 11 March 1765—Mosley Mott orphan of Mosely Mott deced is by the Court bound to George Haynie untill [until] he arrives to the age of Twenty one years, In Consideration of which the s^d Haynie is to learn him the trade of a

Carpenter and Joyner [joiner] & to read, write & cypher [cipher] & to find him sufficient clothing, Diet and Lodging during the s^d Term, But the Clothing the s^d Mott one year & his schooling the said Haynie is to be allowed for out of the Hire of the s^d Orphan's Negro. For the Performance of all which the s^d Haynie with William Taite gent. his security acknowledged themselves bound to the Court in the sum of 5000$^£$ Tob^o. *OB 1762–66, Part 2, 460.*

171. 13 May 1765—An Indenture of apprenticeship from John Garlington to William Blackwell, with the approbation of the Court, was acknowledged by the parties & admitted to Record. *OB 1762–66, Part 2, 490.*

172. 13 May 1765—This Indenture witnesseth, That John Garlington son of William Garlington late of the County of Northumberland and Colony of Virg^a hath put himself and by these presents doth Voluntarily put himself apprentice to William Blackwell of said County mariner, with the Consent of the Court of s^d County, to learn his art, Trade or Mystery, and after the manner of an apprentice to serve him from the day of the date hereof for and during the full term of four years next ensuing, During all of which time he the s^d apprentice his s^d Master shall faithfully serve, his secrets keep, his lawful commands every where gladly obey, he shall do no damage to his s^d Master, nor see it done by others, without giving notice thereof to his s^d Master, he shall not waste his s^d Masters goods nor lend them unlawfully to others, he shall not Contract Matrimony within the s^d Term, at Cards, Dice or any unlawful games he shall not play, whereby his Master shall be damaged, with his own goods or goods of others during the s^d Term without Lycense [license] of his s^d Master, he shall neither buy nor sell, he shall not absent himself day nor night from his s^d Master's Service without his leave nor haunt ale houses, Taverns or play houses, but in all things behave himself as a faithful apprentice ought to be during the s^d Term, and the s^d Master shall use the utmost of his endeavours to Teach or cause to be Instructed the s^d apprentice the s^d art or occupation he now Professeth or followeth, and procure & provide for him the said apprentice sufficient meat and drink fiting [fitting] for an apprentice and will also pay or cause to be paid to the s^d apprentice Forty shillings sterling each year during his apprenticeship which considerations afores^d is allotted by the s^d Master to provide the said apprentice with apperrel [apparel]. And for the true Performance of all & every the s^d Covenants and agreements either of the parties bind themselves unto the other by these presents. In Witness whereof they have interchangeably put their hands and seals this the 10th day of May in the fifth year of his Majesties [Majesty's] reign and in the year of our Lord God 1765. *RB 6, Part 2, 558, 559.*

173. 8 July 1765—John Betts son of Charles Betts deced is by the Court bound to Randolph Mott untill [until] he arrives to the age of Twenty one years. In Consideration of which the s^d Randolph is to give him sufficient schooling & to find him meat, drink, washing & lodging & also to learn him the trade of a Taylor [tailor]. For the Performance of which the s^d Randolph together with

Thomas Downing his security acknowledged themselves bound to the Court in the sum of 5000£ Tob°. *OB 1762–66, Part 2, 518.*

174. 27 July 1765—Will of John Alexander . . . My will and Desire is that my said son (John Shildon Alexander) should go to my friend Soloman Tousan [Townsend] in Worsister [Worcester] County in Maryland, also my will is that my said son should be bound to a house Carpenter and house Joyner [joiner]. . . . *RB 7, 84.*

175. 12 May 1766—Sinah Sebree is by the Court bound to Richard Hudnall untill [until] she arrives at lawfull [lawful] age. In Consideration of which the s^d Hudnall is to learn her the Trade of a Weaver & to read the Bible, also during the s^d Time he is to find her sufficient Diet and Clothing. *OB 1762–66, Part 2, 609.*

176. 12 Aug. 1766—Order'd the Churchwardens of St Stephens Parish for the time being bind James Harcum to Moses Mathews according to law. *OB 1762–66, Part 2, 643.*

177. 26 Oct. 1766—George Curtis orphan of John Curtis is by the Court Bound to William Ball untill [until] he arrives to the age of Twenty one years. In Consideration of which the said Ball is to learn him the Trade of a shoemaker and to Read & write and also to find & provide for the s^d Curtis during the said Term sufficient Clothing, Diet and Lodging. For the due performance of which the said Ball with John Crawley his security acknowledged themselves bound to the Court now sitting in the sum of 5000£ tob°. *OB 1762–66, Part 2, 688.*

178. 10 Nov. 1766—Orderd the Churchwardens of St Stephens Parish for the time being bind the children of Frances Dellsby to Joseph Ball according to law. *OB 1762–66, Part 2, 689.*

179. 11 Nov. 1766—Order'd the Churchwardens of St Stephens Parish for the time being bind out George Coats orphan of John Coats deced. to Hugh James according to law. *OB 1762–66, Part 2, 694.*

180. 8 Dec. 1766—An Indenture of apprenticeship from John Leland to Parish Garner was proved by one of the witnesses thereto subscribed & admitted to Record. *OB 1762–66, Part 2, 710.*

181. 8 Dec. 1766—This Indenture made this 31st of May 1766 Between John Lealand of St Stephens Parish in Northumberland County in the Colony of Virg^a of the one part and Parish Garner of the other part of the same Parish, County & Colony, Witnesseth that the s^d John Lealand doth promise, agree and oblige himself to and with s^d Parish Garner to bind his son Peter Lealand unto the s^d Parish Garner untill [until] he shall attain unto the age of Twenty one years old, and the said Parish Garner doth promise, agree and oblige himself to and with the said John Lealand to find the s^d Peter Lealand, son to the said John Lealand, during his Servitude good sufficient Clothing, meat, drink and Lodging, and to do his Indeavour [endeavor] to learn him to read well & write a plain hand. In witness whereof we have hereunto set our hands & seales [seals] this day & year above mentioned.

John Lealand
Parish Garner

At a Court Held for Northumberland County the 8 day of December 1766. This Indenture of apprenticeship from John Lealand to Parish Garner was Proved by Joseph Wildy one of the witnesses thereto & admitted to Record.

Teste   Thos Jones Clerk Court

RB 7, 6.

182. 8 Dec. 1766—Orderd the Churchwardens of St Stephens Parish for the time being bind out Lucy Fleming Oldham orphan of Lucy West deced by George Turner to Priscilla Harrison according to law. *OB 1762–66, Part 2, 709.*

183. 8 Dec. 1766—William Murphy orphan of Darby Murphy is by the Court & with his Consent bound to Richard Thompson for the Term of Four years from the date hereof. In Consideration of which s^d service the s^d Thompson is to learn him the Trade of a Carpenter or Joyner [joiner] & find for the s^d Murphey during the s^d Term sufficient Cloathing [clothing], Diet and Lodging. For the performance of which the s^d Thompson with Parish Garner and Mathew Neale his securities acknowledged themselves bound with Penalty of 5000 ld. tob^o. *OB 1762–66, Part 2, 711.*

184. 9 Dec. 1766—Order'd the Churchwardens of St Stephens Parish for the time being bind James Roberts orphan of Giles Roberts deced. to Cornelius Daugherty according to law. *OB 1762–66, Part 2, 715.*

185. 9 Dec. 1766—Orderd the Churchwardens of St Stephens Parish for the time being bind out Giles & Rebecca Roberts orphans of Giles Roberts deced according to law. *OB 1762–66, Part 2, 715.*

186. 9 Feb. 1767—Joseph Garlington orphan of Christopher Garlington deced is by the Court bound to Martin Shearman Junr untill [until] he arrives to the age of Twenty one. In Consideration whereof the s^d Martin is to learn him the trade of a Shop Joyner [joiner], and to be Clothed out of the profits of his said Orphan's own Estate. For the Performance of which the s^d Martin together with David Ball Junr acknowledged themselves bound to the Court now setting [sitting] in the sum of 5000 ld. tob^o. *OB 1767–70, 11.*

187. 9 Feb. 1767—Order'd that the Churchwardens of Wicocomoco [Wicomico] Parish for the time being bind out Fortunas Dunaway a bastard child, and Epap^a Newsome orphan of John Newsome deced according to law. *OB 1767–70, 13.*

188. 9 March 1767—William Blincoe orphan of James Blincoe deced, and Vincent Williams orphan of John Williams deced are by the Court bound to John Hornsby for the Term and time of Five years, each from the 25th day of December last past. In Consideration whereof the s^d Hornsby is to learn them the Trade of a Carpenter & Joyner [joiner] and to find them sufficient Clothing, Diet and Lodging. For the due Performance of which he together with Isaac Baysie his security acknowledg'd themselves bound to the Court now sitting in the sum of 5000 ld Tob^o for each orphan. *OB 1767–70, 22.*

189. 10 March 1767—Orderd that the Churchwardens of St. Stephens Parish for the time being bind out William Headon Orphan of Lewis Headon deced to John S. Woodcock according to Law. *OB 1767–70, 27.*

190. 13 April 1767—William Denny Orphan of John Denny deced is by the Court Bound to Randolph Mott untill [until] he arrives at the age of Twenty one. In Consideration whereof the s^d Mott is to learn him the Trade of a Taylor [tailor], & to find him sufficient clothing, Diet & Lodging as also such Education as the Law directs. For the Performance of which the s^d Mott with John Efford his security acknowledged themselves bound to the Court now setting [sitting] in the sum of 5000 ld tob^o. *OB 1767–70, 30.*

191. 13 April 1767—Nancy Sebree orphan of John Sebree deced is by the Court bound to Randolph Mott & his wife untill [until] she arrives to the age of eighteen years. In Consideration whereof they are to learn her to Read, sew and spin & to find her sufficient Clothing, Diet & Lodging. For the Performance of which the s^d Mott with John Cralle Junr his security acknowledg'd themselves bound to the Court now setting [sitting] in the sum of 5000 ld. Tob^o. *OB 1767–70, 30.*

192. 14 July 1767—Orderd that the Churchwardens of St Stephens Parish for the time being bind Hannah McCalley orphan of John McCalley deced to John Cralle Junr according to law. *OB 1767–70, 94.*

193. 10 Aug. 1767—James Nutt orphan of Benjamin Nutt deced is by the Court bound to Major Bickerdick untill [until] he arrives at the age of Twenty one years. In Consideration of which the s^d Bickerdick is to give him one years schooling, to learn him the trade of a Taylor [tailor], & also during the s^d Term to find him sufficient clothing, Diet and Lodging, for the due performance of which the s^d Bickerdick together with Mark Harding his security acknowledg'd themselves bound to the Court now setting [sitting] in the sum of 5000 ld. tob^o. *OB 1767–70, 101.*

194. 9 Nov. 1767—Thomas Nutt orphan of Farnifold Nutt deced. is by the Court bound to Farnifold Nutt untill [until] he arrives at the age of Twenty one years, on consideration of which the said Farnif^d Nutt is to learn him the trade of a shoemaker and to find for him during the s^d term sufficient Diet, Cloathing [clothing] and lodging. For the due performance of which the s^d Farnifold together with John Rogers his security acknowledged themselves [bound] to this Court in the sum of 5000 ld. tob^o. *OB 1767–70, 135.*

195. 12 Jan. 1768—Orderd that the Churchwardens of St Stephens Parish for the time being bind out the Orphans of John Neasome & Margaret Reason deced according to law. *OB 1767–70, 145.*

196. 8 Feb. 1768—Order'd that the Churchwardens of Wiccomoco [Wicomico] Parish for the time being bind Cornelius Sullivan to John Beane according to Law. *OB 1767–70, 153.*

197. 8 Feb. 1768—Richard Kellem orphan of Richard Kellem deced is by the Court bound to Mark Harding untill [until] he arrives at the age of Twenty one years. In Consideration of which the s^d Harding is to learn him the Trade of a Taylor [tailor], and also during the s^d Term to find & provide for the s^d Richard sufficient Cloathing [clothing], Diet and Lodging. For the Performance of which the s^d Harding together with William Parrett & Onefiphorus Harvey his securities acknowledged themselves bound to the Court now setting [sitting] in the sum of 5000 ld. tob^o. *OB 1767–70, 154.*

198. 8 Feb. 1768—Ephraim Hughlett & John Hughlett Orphans of Nicholas Hughlett deced are by the Court bound to Mark Harding untill [until] they severally arrive at the age of Twenty one years. In Consideration of which the s^d Harding is to learn them the Taylors [tailor's] trade, and also during the s^d Term, to find and provide for the s^d Ephraim & John, sufficient Cloathing [clothing], Diet and Lodging. For the performance of which the s^d Harding together with William Parrett and Onefiphorus Harvey his securities acknowledged themselves bound to the Court now setting [sitting] in the sum of 10,000 ld. tob^o. *OB 1767–70, 154.*

199. 8 Feb. 1768—An Indenture of apprenticeship from James Mason to John Malady was proved by the witnesses thereto subscribed & admitted to record. *OB 1767–70, 156.*

200. 6 Feb. 1768—This indenture made the sixth day of February in the Eighth year of the Reign of our Sovereign Lord George the third by the grace of God of great Britain, France and Ireland King Defender of the faith etc. and in the year of our Lord Christ 1768. Between James Mason of the Parish of St Stephens and County of Northumberland of the one part, and John Malady of the same Parish and County Blacksmith of the other part, Witnesseth that James Mason for the Consideration hereafter mentioned and expressed Doe [do] and by these Presents put and Bind himself an Apprentice and Servant unto the said John Malady for and during the full and Term of Four Years, from the 29 day of October last past. All which Term and Time of four years the said James Mason his said Master shall faithfully serve in any lawfull Imployment [employment]. He shall not absent himself from his s^d Master's service at any time during the said Term without the Consent of his said Master nor Contract Matrimony, but in all things truly, faithfully and Honestly obey and serve his said Master during the Term and time aforesaid. In Consideration whereof the said John Malady doth by these presents agree and oblige himself to Teach and Instruct or Cause to be Taught or Instructed his said apprentice in the Art, Trade, or Mistery [mystery] of a Blacksmith, and also during the said Term and Time of four years as aforesaid, to find and Provide for his said Apprentice or servant, sufficient Clothing, Diet, washing and Lodging. In Witness whereof the parties to these presents hath Interchangeably set their hands and seals the day, month and year above written.

            his
         James Mason
           mark
           his
        John Malady
          mark

RB 7, 175.

201. 14 March 1768—John Winter Orphan of William Winter deced is by the Court & by his own Consent bound to John Hunton for the term of two years from the date hereof. In Consideration of wch he is to teach & Instruct him in the Art & Trade of a Shop Joyner [joiner]. For the Performance of which the s^d Hunton with William Blackerby his security acknowledged themselves bound to the Court now sitting in the sum of 5000 ld tob^o. *OB 1767–70, 168.*

202. 11 April 1768—Richard Thomas with the approbation of the Court hereby binds his son George Thomas an apprentice unto Randolph Mott untill [until] he arrives to the age of Twenty one years. In Consideration of which the said Mott is to learn him the trade of a Taylor [tailor] and to find for the s^d George all necessarys [necessaries] as by law is required. For the Performance of which the s^d Randolph acknowledges himself bound to the Court now setting [sitting] in the Penalty of 5000 ld. tob^o. *OB 1767–70, 179.*

203. 11 April 1768—James Webb orphan of James Webb deced is by the Court and with the Consent of his mother, bound to Jesse Pitman untill [until] he arrives to the age of Twenty one years. In Consideration of which the s^d Pitman is to learn him the trade of a weaver and to Read, Write & Cypher [cipher], as also to find for the s^d James all other necessaries as is by the law required. For the Performance of which the s^d Pitman with Saml Eskridge and Robert Clarke his Securities acknowledged themselves bound to the Court now setting [sitting] in the Penalty of 5000 ld. tob^o. *OB 1767–70, 180.*

204. 12 Sept. 1768—George Danks orphan of George Danks deced who was born the 27th of April 1755, is by the Court bound to William Morton untill [until] he arrives at the age of Twenty one years. In Consideration of the s^d Morton is to learn him the Trade of a Taylor [tailor] & to read, write & Cypher [cipher] as also to find him sufficient clothing, Diet & Lodging. For the due performance of which the s^d Morton with William Eskridge his security acknowledged themselves bound to the Court now setting [sitting] in the sum of 5000 ld. tob°. *OB 1767–70, 290.*

205. 11 Oct. 1768—Fleet Chilton and John Chilton orphans of Stephen Chilton deced. is by the Court bound to Benjamin Clarke, the said Fleet for the term of four years & the said John for the term of five years from the date hereof. In consideration of which the said Clarke is to learn them the trade of a Carpenter & Joyner [joiner] to pay each of them three pounds cur. [current] money per annum in lieu of clothing & to find them sufficient diet and lodging, Judith Chilton their mother agreeing to find them clothing. For the due performance of which the s^d Clarke with John Williams his security acknowledged themselves bound to the Court now setting [sitting] in the sum of 5000 ld. tobacco. *OB 1767–70, 310.*

206. 12 Dec. 1768—Order'd that the Churchwardens of St Stephens Parish for the time being bind out Rodham Tullis orphan of John Tullis deced to James Courtney according to Law. *OB 1767–70, 321.*

207. 9 Jan. 1769—Rodham Kenner Cralle Orphan of Rodham Cralle deced is by the Court bound to William Grayson untill [until] he arrives at the age of Twenty one years. In Consideration of which the s^d Grayson is to learn him the Trade of a Carpenter & Joyner [joiner], to read, write & Cypher [cipher] & also find him during the s^d Term Sufficient Clothing, Diet & Lodging. For the due Performance of which the s^d Grayson with William Eskridge & William Lewis his securities acknowledged themselves bound to the Court now sitting in the Penalty of 5000 ld. tob°. *OB 1767–70, 328.*

208. 13 Feb. 1769—Giles Sydnor Orphan of Epaphroditus Sydnor deced is by the Court & with the Consent of himself & guardian bound to Martin Shearman Junr untill [until] he arrives at the age of Twenty one years. In Consideration of which the s^d Shearman is to learn him the trade of a Shop Joyner [joiner] & to find him sufficient Diet & Lodging (his guardian agreeing to find him sufficient cloathing [clothing] & pay his levy). For the due performance of which the s^d Shearman wth John Sydnor his security acknowledged themselves bound to the Court now setting [sitting] in the Penalty of 5000 ld tob°. *OB 1767–70, 331.*

209. 13 Feb. 1769—Meredith Nelms Orphan of Aaron Nelms deced is by the Court bound to John Hornsby untill [until] he arrives to the age of Twenty one years. In Consideration of which the s^d John is to learn him the Trade of a Carpenter & Joyner [joiner] & to learn him to read, write & Cypher [cipher] & to find him sufficient Clothing, Diet & Lodging. For the due Performance of which the s^d John with Henry Boggess his security, acknowledged themselves bound to the Court now setting [sitting] in the Penalty of 5,000 ld tob°. *OB 1767–70, 332.*

210. 13 March 1769—Thomas Marsh orphan of John Marsh deced. is by the Court bound to Peter Marsh untill [until] he arrives at the age of twenty one years. In Consideration of which the s^d Peter is to learn him to read, write & cypher [cipher], and the Trade of a Carpenter, also to find him sufficient diet, clothing and lodging. For the performance of which he with William Nutt his security acknowledg'd themselves bound to the Court now setting [sitting] in the sum of 5000 ld. tobacco. *OB 1767–70, 337.*

211. 13 March 1769—Order'd that the Churchwardens of St Stephens Parish for the time being bind Michael Molony son of Michael Molony to John Hodges according to law. *OB 1767–70, 340.*

212. 10 April 1769—John Straughan orphan of David Straughan is by the Court bound to William Grayson untill [until] he arrives at full age. In Consideration of which the said Grayson is to learn him the trade of a Carpenter & Joyner [joiner], to learn him to read, write & Cypher [cipher] & to find & provide for the s^d Jn° Straughan during the said term sufficient Clothing, Diet & lodging. For the due Performance of which the said William Grayson with Kenner Cralle & William Lewis securities acknowledged themselves bound to the Court now sitting in the Penalty of 5000 ld. of tobacco. *OB 1767–70, 348.*

213. 10 April 1769—An Indenture of Apprenticeship from Adam Bussell to John Malady was acknowledg'd by the parties & admitted to record. *OB 1767–70, 353.*

214. 10 April 1769—This Indenture made the 10th day of April in the Ninth year of the Reign of our Sovereign Lord George the Third by the grace of God of Great Britain, France & Ireland King Defender of the faith etc. and in the year our Lord Christ 1769 Between Adam Bussell of the Parish of St Stephens and County of Northumberland of the one part, and John Malady of the same Parish and County Blacksmith of the other part, Witnesseth that the said Adam Bussell for the Consideration hereafter mentioned and expressed, Doe [do] and by these Presents Doth put and Bind himself an apprentice and servant unto the said John Malady for and during the full Term of five years from the first day of November last, all which Term and time of five years the said Adam Bussell his said Master shall faithfully serve in any Lawfull Imployment [employment]. He shall not absent himself from his said Master's service at any time during the s^d Term without the Consent of his said Master, nor Contract Matrimony, but in all things, truly faithfully and Honestly obey and serve his said Master during the Term and Time aforesaid. In Consideration whereof the s^d John Malady doth by these presents agree and oblige himself to Teach and Instruct or Cause to be Taught or Instructed his said apprentice in the Art, Trade or Mistery [mystery] of a Blacksmith, and also during the s^d Term and time of five years as afores^d to find and Provide for his s^d apprentice or servant sufficient, clothing, Diet, Washing and lodging. In Witness whereof the parties to these presents hath Interchangeably set their hands and seals the day, month and year above written.

his
Adam   Bussell
mark
his
John   Malady
mark

RB 7, 345.

215. 8 May 1769—Order'd that the Churchwardens of St Stephens Parish for the time being bind William Dameron Dawson to John Dawson according to Law. *OB 1767–70, 368.*

216. 12 June 1769—George Betts orphan of Charles Betts deced is by the Court bound to John Betts untill [until] he arrives at the age of Twenty one. In Consideration thereof the s^d John is to learn the s^d George the trade of a Taylor [tailor], to read, write & Cypher [cipher] & also to find him sufficient Clothing, Diet & Lodging. For the due performance of which the s^d John with Thomas Hudnall his security acknowledged themselves bound to the Court now setting [sitting] in the sum of 5000 ld. tob^o. *OB 1767–70, 385.*

217. 9 Oct. 1769—James Walker son of John Walker is by the Court bound to Benjamin Clarke for the term of five years from Xmas next. In Consideration of which the s^d Clarke is to learn him to read, write & cypher [cipher], & the trade of a Carpenter & Joyner [joiner] as also to find for the s^d Walker sufficient diet, lodging & apperil [apparel]. For the due performance of which the s^d Clarke with Thomas Reid his security acknowledged themselves bound to the Court now setting [sitting] in the sum of 5,000 ld. tobacco. *OB 1767–70, 418.*

218. 13 Nov. 1769—Winefred Walker orphan of John Walker deced. is by the Court bound to Jane Humphris untill [until] she is of full age. In Consideration of which the s^d Jane is to learn her to read, sew & spin, as also to provide for her sufficient Diet, Lodging & Clothing. For the due performance of which she with Joseph Hudnall her security acknowledg'd themselves bound to the Court now setting [sitting] in the sum of 5000 ld. tobacco. *OB 1767–70, 433.*

219. 12 Feb. 1770—George Webb orphan of William Webb deced. is by the Court bound to George Smither untill [until] he arrives to the age of Twenty one years. In Consideration of which the s^d Smither is to learn him to read, write & cypher [cipher] & the Trade of a Taylor [tailor], as also to find him sufficient Clothing, Diet & Lodging. For the due performance of which the s^d George Smither together with Saml Eskridge his security acknowledged themselves bound to the Court now setting [sitting] in the sum of 5000 ld. tob^o. *OB 1767–*

70, 443.

220. 12 March 1770—Indenture of Apprenticeship from Daniel McCoy to Randolph Mott was acknowledg'd by the parties, and admitted to Record. *OB 1767–70, 447.*

221. 12 Feb. 1770—This Indenture made this 12 Day of February in the year of our Lord Christ one Thousand Seven hundred and Seventy & in the Tenth year of the Reign of our Sovereign Lord George the third of Great Britain, France & Ireland King Defender of the faith etc. Between Randolph Mott of Northumberland County & Colony of Virginia Taylor [tailor] of the one part, and Daniel McCoy of the County and Colony aforesaid of the other part Witnesseth that the said Randolph Mott for the Consideration of the said Daniel McCoy's serving him the said Randolph Mott Two years to Begin and Commence the first day of January last past, The said Randolph Mott doth agree and oblige himself his heirs etc. to learn the said Daniel McCoy the Trade and Occupation of a Taylor [tailor] or at least to do his true Indeavour [endeavor] to learn the said Trade & to find him in good wholesome Victuals, Lodging & Clothing During his said Daniel McCoy's apprenticeship and to use in a Human and Christian like manner During all which Time the said Daniel McCoy is to behave himself well and to obey all his said Master's Just and Lawfull [lawful] Commands and to do any sort of Lawfull [lawful] Business or employment that his said Master shall think Proper to sett [set] him the said Daniel McCoy about, and he is not to absent himself from his said Master's Business during his said apprenticeship nor to Mary [marry] or to comitt [commit] Fornication or a Dultary [adultery] nor Frequent Publick [public] Houses nor Follow Unlawful gaiming [gaming] without his said Master's Consent. In Witness whereof the said Randolph Mott and the said Daniel McCoy hath hereunto sett [set] there [their] hands and affixed their seals the Day and year above written.

           Randolph Mott
           Daniel McCoy

RB 7, 469, 470.

222. 12 March 1770—Maximillian Haynie orphan of Abraham Haynie deced. is by the court bound to John Flynt untill [until] he arrives to the age of Twenty one years. In Consideration of which the s^d Flynt is to learn him to read, write & cypher [cipher] & the Trade of a Taylor [tailor] as also to provide for him sufficient Clothing, Diet & Lodging. For the performance of which the s^d Flynt with Thomas Smith & James Temple his Securities acknowledg^d themselves bound to the Court now setting [sitting] in the sum of 5000 ld. tob^o. *OB 1767–70, 449.*

223. 12 March 1770—James Harcum orphan of Thomas Harcum deced is by the Court bound to Thomas Smith untill [until] he arrives to the age of Twenty one years. In Consideration of which the said Smith is to learn him to read, write & Cypher [cipher] & the trade of a shoemaker, as also to find him sufficient clothing, Diet & Lodging. For the performance of which he with John Flynt & William Smith his securities acknowledged themselves bound to the Court now setting [sitting] in the sum of 5000 ld. tob^o. *OB 1767–70, 451.*

224. 12 March 1770—Molly Walker Daughter to John Walker is by the Court bound to Thomas Walker untill [until] she arrives at full age. In Consideration of which the s^d Thomas Walker is to learn her to Read & to find her sufficient Clothing, Diet & Lodging. For the due performance of which he with Edwin Farned his security acknowledged themselves bound to the Court now sitting in the sum of 5000 ld. tob^o. *OB 1767–70, 451.*

225. 9 April 1770—Order'd that the Churchwardens of Wicoc^o [Wicomico] Parish for the time being bind out the Orphans of Michael Taylor & Robert Miller deced. according to law. *OB 1767–70, 461.*

226. 10 April 1770—Mary Danks orphan of George Danks is by the Court bound to Rebecca Craine untill [until] she arrives at full age. In Consideration of which the said Rebecca is to learn her to read, & to find her sufficient Clothing, Diet & Lodging. For the due performance of which she with John S. Woodcock acknowledged themselves bound to the Court now sitting in the sum of 5000 ld tob^o. *OB 1767–70, 476.*

227. 15 May 1770—Order'd that the Churchwardens of St Stephens Parish for the time being bind out Yarrot Hughlett orphan of Nicholas Hughlett deced according to law. *OB 1767–70, 495.*

228. 11 June 1770—Order'd the Churchwardens of Wicoc^o [Wicomico] Parish for the time being bind out Nicholas Hill orphan of John Hill deced. to John Smither according to law. *OB 1767–70, 502.*

229. 9 July 1770—John Smith orphan of Betty Smith deced is by the Court bound to John Hornsby untill [until] he arrives at the age of Twenty one years. In Consideration of which the said Hornsby is to learn him to read, write & Cypher [cipher] & the trade of a carpenter, as also to find him sufficient Clothing, Diet & Lodging. For the due performance of which he the s^d Hornsby with John Cralle j^r his security acknowledged themselves bound to the Court now setting [sitting] in the sum of 5000 ld tob^o. *OB 1770–73, 7.*

230. 8 Oct. 1770—Rodham Tulles orphan of John Tulles deced. is by the Court bound to George Haynie until he arrives to the age of Twenty one years. In consideration of which the said Haynie is to learn him the trade of a carpenter & Joyner [joiner] & to read, write and Cypher [cipher] as also during the s^d term, to find him sufficient Clothing, Diet and Lodging according to Law. For the due performance of which the s^d George Haynie with George Smither & Edwin Farned his securities acknowledged themselves bound to the Court now setting [sitting] in the sum of 5000 ld. tobacco. *OB 1770–73, 43.*

231. 14 Jan. 1771—Mathew Bussell orphan of Phillip Bussell deced is by the Court bound to Francis Kenner, untill [until] he arrives to the age of Twenty one years. In Consideration whereof the said Kenner is to learn him to read, write, & cypher [cipher] & the Trade of a Shoemaker, & to find for him sufficient Diet, Lodging & Clothing. For the due performance of which he with John Hornsby his security acknowledged themselves bound to the Court now setting [sitting] in 5000£ tob°. *OB 1770–73, 68.*

232. 14 Jan. 1771—Winter Hughlett orphan of Thomas Hughlett deced is by the Court bound to Peter Beane untill [until] he arrives to the age of Twenty one. In Consideration of which the s^d Beane is to learn him to read, write & Cypher [cipher], & the trade of a Taylor [tailor], as also to find for him sufficient Clothing, Diet & Lodging. For the performance of which he with George Beane & Mayes Fletcher his Securities, acknowledged themselves bound to the Court now setting [sitting] in the sum of 5000£ tob°. *OB 1770–73, 71.*

233. 11 March 1771—Thomas Gaskins Orphan of Josiah Gaskins deced is by the Court bound to James Lewis untill [until] he arrives to the age of Twenty one years. In Consideration of which the s^d Ja^s Lewis is to learn him to read, write, & Cypher [cipher] & the Trade of a house carpenter, as also to find for him sufficient Clothing, Diet & Lodging. For the due Performance of which he with William Downing his security acknowledged themselves bound to the Court now sitting in the sum of 5000£ tob°. *OB 1770–73, 73.*

234. 11 March 1771—Thomas Palmer orphan of Nargail Palmer deced is by the Court bound to Lott Palmer untill [until] he arrives to the age of Twenty one years. In Consideration of which the s^d Lott is to Learn him to read, write & Cypher [cipher] & the trade of a Bricklayer, as also to find him sufficient Clothing, Diet & Lodging. For the performance of which he with Moses Sutton his security, acknowledged themselves bound to the Court now setting [sitting] in 5000 ld. tob°. *OB 1770–73, 75.*

235. 10 June 1771—George Betts Orphan of Charles Betts deced. is by the Court bound to Randolph Mott untill [until] he arrives to the age of Twenty one years. In Consideration of which the s^d Mott is to learn him the Taylor's [tailor's] trade & to read, write & Cypher [cipher] according to law, as also to find & provide for the s^d Betts sufficient Clothing, Diet & Lodging. For the due performance of which he with Thomas Hudnall his security acknowledged themselves bound to the Court now setting [sitting] in the sum of 5,000 ld. Tob°. *OB 1770–73, 144.*

236. 11 June 1771—Spencer Hill orphan of Spencer Hill deced. is by the Court bound to John Sutton untill [until] he arrives to the age of Twenty one years. In Consideration of which the s^d Sutton is to learn him the trade of a Carpenter, to read, right [write] & cypher [cipher], as also to find & provide for him sufficient Clothing, Diet & Lodging. For the due performance of which the s^d Sutton, with Thomas Downing his security, acknowledged themselves bound to the Court now setting [sitting] in the sum of 5000 ld. tob°. *OB 1770–73, 149.*

237. 11 Nov. 1771—William Wilday orphan of Frederick Wilday deced is by the Court Bound to Wm Morton untill [until] he arrives to the age of Twenty one years. In consideration of which the s^d Morton is to learn him the trade of a Taylor [tailor], as also to find him sufficient Clothing, Diet and Lodging for the due Performance of which the s^d William Morton together with George Smither his Security acknowledged themselves bound to the Court now sitting in the sum of _____ [no amount shown]. *OB 1770–73, 218.*

238. 10 Dec. 1771—John Danks Orphan of George Danks deced is by the Court bound to Wm Smither untill [until] he arrives to the age of Twenty one years in Consideration of which the s^d William Smither is to learn him to read, right [write] & cypher [cipher] and the Trade of a Taylor [tailor] as also to find for him sufficient Clothing, Diet and Lodging for the Due Performance of which he with Wm Gilburt his security acknowledged themselves bound to the Court now setting [sitting] in the sum of 5000$^£$ tob°. *OB 1770–73, 245.*

239. 13 Jan. 1772—Stephen Crain orphan of Stephen Crain deced is by the Court bound to Randolph Mott untill [until] he arrives to the age of Twenty one years in consideration of which the s^d Randolph Mott is to learn him to read, right [write] and Cypher [cipher] and the Trade of a Taylor [tailor] as also to find for him sufficient Clothing, Diet and Lodging for the due performance of which he with Robert Hening & Leroy Pullen his Securities acknowledged themselves bound to the Court now sitting in the sum of 5000$^£$ tob°. *OB 1770–73, 249.*

240. 13 Jan. 1772—Henage Sebastian Orphan of Jos. Sebastian deced is by the Court bound to George Astin untill [until] he arrives to the age of Twenty one Years. In Consideration whereof the said Astain is to learn him to read, right [write] and Cypher [cipher] and the Trade of a bricklayer & to find for him sufficient Diet, Lodging and Cloathing [clothing] for the due performance of which he together with Joseph Power his security acknowledged themselves bound to the Court now sitting in 5000$^£$ tob°. *OB 1770–73, 252.*

241. 9 March 1772—William Everitt orphan of Raw. Everitt deced is by the Court Bound to Randolph Mott untill [until] he arrives to the age of Twenty one years in consideration whereof the s^d Mott is to learn him to read, writ [write] and Cypher [cipher] & the trade of a Taylor [tailor] & to find for him sufficient Diet, Lodging & Cloathing [clothing] for the Due performance of which he with Thomas Downing his Security acknowledged themselves bound to the Court now sitting in 5000$^£$ tob°. *OB 1770–73, 260.*

242. 9 March 1772—Thomas Gill orphan of Thomas Gill deced is by the Court bound to John Abby untill [until] he arrives to the age of Twenty one years in consideration whereof the s^d Abby is to learn him to read, write & cypher [cipher] & the trade of a Taylor [tailor] & to find for him sufficient diet, Lodging and Cloathing [clothing] for the due performance of which he with William Parker Garner his security acknowledged themselves bound to the Court now sitting in 5000£ tob°. *OB 1770–73, 261.*

243. 13 April 1772—James Harcum orphan of Thomas Harcum deced is by the Court Bound to George Smither untill [until] he arrives to the age of Twenty one years. In consideration of which the s^d Smither is to learn him the trade of a Taylor [tailor], to Read, Wright [write] and Cypher [cipher] as also to find and provide for him sufficient Cloathing [clothing], diet and Lodging. For the due Performance of which the s^d Smither with Joseph Harcum his security acknowledged themselves Bound to the Court now sitting in the sum of five thousand Pounds of Tob°. *OB 1770–73, 277.*

244. 13 April 1772—Ordered Churchwardens of Wicomoco [Wicomico] Parish for the time being bind out Richard Edwards, Tarpley Webb, Joseph Pitman, Darcus Pitman, Nancy Reason & Nancy Short poor Orphans according to law. *OB 1770–73, 278.*

245. 14 April 1772—Jane Mills having complained to this Court against Nathl Wilson her master for ill usage on hearing the Parties, It is that she serve her sd. Master two months after her former time of service is expired and that the sheriff carry her home to her s^d master. *OB 1770–73, 293.*

246. 11 May 1772—Ep^a Timberlake is by the Court bound unto Thomas Hathaway untill [until] he arrives to the age of Twenty one years in Consideration of which the said Hathaway is to learn him the trade of a saddle [saddler] and to Read, right [write] and Cypher [cipher] as also During the s^d Term to find him sufficient Cloathing [clothing], diet and Lodging according to Law for the due performance of which the s^d Thomas Hathaway together with Martin Shearman his Security acknowledged themselves bound unto the Court now sitting in the sum of 5000£ tob°. *OB 1770–73, 304.*

247. 11 May 1772—William McGoon Orphan of John McGoon deced is by the Court bound to John Hall j^r untill [until] he arrives to the age of Twenty one years. In Consideration thereof the s^d Hall is to learn him to Read, write and Cypher [cipher] and the trade of a Carpenter and to find for him sufficient Diet, Lodging and Cloathing [clothing], of the due Performance of which he together with James Claughton his security [have] acknowledged themselves bound unto the Court now sitting in 5000£ tob°. *OB 1770–73, 312.*

248. 11 May 1772—On the motion of Henage Sebastian against George Astain his Master for his Freedom it is the opinion of the Court that he is of full age and is Discharged accordingly. *OB 1770–73, 313.*

249.   9 June 1772—Ordered that the Churchwardens of Wiccomoco [Wicomico] Parish bind out Mary Weaver according to law. *OB 1770–73, 378.*

250.   14 Sept. 1772—John Summors orphan is by the Court bound to Roger Dameron untill [until] he arrives to the age of Twenty one years. In consideration whereof the s^d Dameron is to learn him the trade of a carpenter and joyner [joiner] and to find him sufficient cloathing [clothing], Diet and Lodging as also such education as the law directs for the Performance of which the s^d Roger Dameron with Wm Dameron his security acknowledged themselves bound to the Court now setting [sitting] in the sum of 5000 lds. tobacco. [In the index of the Order Book, the name is Summers.] *OB 1770–73, 437.*

251.   15 Sept. 1772—Upon the motion of Josiah Gaskins against John Betts for ill usage on hearing each party, It is considered by the Court that the s^d Betts give Security for his good Behaviour for the space of one whole year the Principal in twenty pounds and Security in £10 which he refusing to doe [do], It is ordered that he be Committed to goal [jail] untill [until] such security be given. *OB 1770–73, 442.*

252.   9 Nov. 1772—Matthew Bussell orphan of Phillip Bussell deced. is by the Court bound to Thomas Smith untill [until] he arrives to the age of Twenty one years. In consideration whereof the s^d Smith is to learn him to write, cypher [cipher] and Read & the trade of a Shoemaker & to find him Sufficient Diet, Lodging and Cloathing [clothing]. For the Due performance of which he with Jno Blincoe his security acknowledged themselves bound to the Court now sitting in the sum of 5000$^£$ tobacco. *OB 1770–73, 462.*

253.   14 Dec. 1772—William Edwards orphan of John Edwards Deced is by the Court bound to Randolph Mott untill [until] he arrives to the age of Twenty one years. In Consideration whereof he the s^d Mott is to learn him to read, write & Cypher [cipher] and the trade of a Taylor [tailor] and to find for him Sufficient Diet, Lodging & Cloathing [clothing]. For the due performance of which he together with Thomas Downing and Robt Hening his Securitys [securities] acknowledged themselves bound to the Court now sitting in 5000 tob^o. *OB 1770–73, 466.*

254.   11 Jan. 1773—Wm Crowther orphan of James Crowther Deced is by the Court bound to Henry Ober for four years. In consideration of which the s^d Ober is to learn him Navigation and to give him one Years Schooling & Sufficient Diet, Lodging and cloathing [clothing] for the due performance of which he together with Wm Lewis & Robt Crowther his Securities entered into and acknowledged their bond to the Court now sitting in the Penalty of 5000$^£$ tob^o. *OB 1770–73, 485.*

255.   10 May 1773—Richard Thomas not appearing, on Complaint of Joseph Hudnall for ill usage, it is order'd that an alias attachment Issue against him returnable to the next Court. *OB 1773–83, 2.*

256. 13 March 1775—On the motion of Thomas Gaskins an apprentice to James Lewis for ill usuage [usage] it is order'd the sherriff [sheriff] summon the s^d James Lewis to appear at the next court. *OB 1773–83, 234.*

257. 9 Aug. 1773—Upon complaint of James Walker against his master Benjamin Clarke for freedom on hearing the witnesses, it is the opinion of the Court that the s^d Walker is of full age whereupon he is discharged from the service. *OB 1773–83, 56.*

258. 13 Sept. 1773—Whiden Benn orphan of Arthur Benn deced is by the Court bound to Charles Haynie until he arrives to the age of Twenty one years. In consideration of which the s^d Haynie is to learn him to sail and manage a vessel in the Bay & rivers, & to give him such Education, Board & Clothing as the law requires. For the due performance of which the s^d Chas Haynie together with James Lewis his security acknowledges themselves bound to the Court now setting [sitting] in the sum of 5000 ld tob^o. *OB 1773–83, 71.*

259. 15 Feb. 1774—Thomas Sutton is by the Court bound to John Webb untill [until] he arrives to the age of Twenty one years, in Consideration of which service, the said Webb is to learn him the trade of a Carpenter & Joyner [joiner], & to give him such Education, Clothing, Diet & Lodging as is by law required. For the due performance of which the s^d John Webb with John Haynie his Security acknowledge themselves bound to the Court now sitting in the sum of 5,000 ld tob^o. *OB 1773–83, 126.*

260. 14 March 1774—Order'd that the Churchwardens of Wicomoco [Wicomico] Parish for the time being Bind out Richard Edwards, Patty Short, John Dowlin & Alice Slack Hall according to Law. *OB 1773–83, 128.*

261. 13 June 1774—Order'd that the Churchwardens of Wicomoco [Wicomico] Parish for the time being bind out Ezekiel Blanch according to law. *OB 1773–83, 207.*

262. 10 Oct. 1774—Order'd that the Churchwardens of Wicomoco [Wicomico] Parish for the time being bind out Thomas Sullivant orphan of Cornelius Sullivant deced according to law. *OB 1773–83, 221.*

263. 14 Nov. 1774—Order'd that the Churchwardens of St Stephens Parish for the time being bind out Thomas Wilkins, Peter Wilkins, John Dykes, Richard Dykes, Pendly Dykes, Robert Dykes, William Dykes & Thomas Dykes, according to Law. *OB 1773–83, 226.*

264. 13 Feb. 1775—James Thomas orphan of Aggy Thomas is by the Court bound to John Sebree untill [until] he arrives to the age of Twenty one years. In consideration of which the s^d Jno Sebree is to learn him the Trade of a Bricklayer and to find for him during the said Term such Diet, Clothing & Lodging & give him such education as the Law directs. For the due performance of which the s^d Sebree together with William Betts and William Packet his Securities acknowledged themselves bound to the Court now sitting in the sum of 5000 ld tob^o. *OB 1773–83, 232.*

265. 13 March 1775—On the motion of Thomas Gaskins an apprentice to James Lewis for ill usuage [usage], it is order'd the sherriff [sheriff] summon the s^d James Lewis to appear at the next Court. *OB 1773–83, 234.*

266. 10 April 1775—The complaint made by Thomas Gaskins against Master James Lewis for ill usage is dismissed. *OB 1773–83, 236.*

267. 10 July 1775—Jordan Betts a bastard Child is by the Court bound to William Morton untill [until] he arrives to the age of Twenty one years, in Consideration of which the s^d Morton is to learn him the Trade of a Taylor [tailor], and to find for him during the said Term such Diet, Clothing & Lodging, & give him such Education as the law directs. For the due performance of which the s^d Morton together with Bridgar Haynie his Security acknowledged themselves bound to the Court now sitting in the sum of 5000 ld tob^o. *OB 1773–83, 237.*

268. 10 July 1775—Order'd that the Churchwardens of Wicomoco [Wicomico] Parish for the time being bind out Richard Craine son of James Craine & John Robuck orphan of William Robuck deced according to law. *OB 1773–83, 238.*

269. 12 Feb. 1776—By consent of Betty Schofield mother of Thomas Cammell, the said Thomas is by the Court bound to George Smither untill [until] he arrives to the age of twenty years, on Consideration of which the said Smither is to learn him the Trade of a Taylor [tailor] & find him sufficient Diet and Lodging, but no cloths [clothes], neither is he to pay any Freedom dues. For the performance the s^d Smither together with Thomas Downing & John Rogers his securities acknowledged themselves bound to the Court now setting [sitting] in 5000 ld. tobacco. *OB 1773–83, 252.*

270. 12 Feb. 1776—Thomas Harding Orphan of Mark Harding deced is by the Court bound to John Hughlett untill [until] he arrives to the age of Twenty one years, in Consideration of which the s^d Hughlett is to learn him the Trade of a Taylor [tailor] & to find him Sufficient Cloathing [clothing], Diet & Lodging & give him such Learning as the Law directs. For the due performance of which the s^d Hughlett together with William Barrott & William Hughlett his Securities acknowledged themselves bound to the Court now setting [sitting] in 5000 ld tob^o. *OB 1773–83, 253.*

271. 11 March 1776—William Curtis orphan of Betty Dudley deced is by the

Court bound to George Smither untill [until] he arrives to the age of Twenty one years, in Consideration of which the said Geo. Smither is to learn him the Trade of a Taylor [tailor], and to find for him sufficient Clothing, Diet & Lodging, & give him such education as the law directs. For the due performance of which the s^d Smither together with William Eskridge his Security acknowledged themselves bound to the Court now setting [sitting] in 5000 ld tob^o. *OB 1773–83, 256.*

272. 13 May 1776—James Webb orphan of Joseph Webb deced is by the Court bound to Martin Shearman untill [until] he arives [arrives] to the age of Twenty one years, in consideration of which the said Martin Shearman is to learn him the trade of a Carpenter & House Joyner [joiner] & to find for him during the said Term such Clothing, Diet & Lodging & give him such Education as the law requires. For the due performance of which the s^d Martin with Nicholas Pope his Security acknowledged themselves bound to the Court now setting [sitting] in the sum of 5000 ld tob^o. *OB 1773–83, 259.*

273. 14 Oct. 1776—Samuel Templeman Orphan of James Templeman deced. is by the Court bound to Randolph Mott untill [until] he arrives to the age of Twenty one years, in consideration of which the s^d Randolph Mott is to learn him the Trade of a Taylor [tailor] & give him such education, Clothing, Diet and Lodging as the Law in such cases requirs [requires]. For the due performance of which he the s^d Randolph together with Thomas Downing and Charles Copedge his securities acknowledged themselves bound to the Court now setting [sitting] in the sum of 5000 ld. tobacco. *OB 1773–83, 270.*

274. 10 March 1777—Betty Spry Orphan of James Spry deced. is by the Court bound to Winder Kenner gent. untill [until] she arrives to the age of eighteen years, in consideration whereof the s^d Winder Kenner obliges himself to give her such Schooling, Clothing, Diet & Lodging as the law in such cases require [requires]. *OB 1773–83, 285.*

275. 9 June 1777—Hannah Bartes Orphan of George Bartes is by the Court bound to Thomas Williams untill [until] she arrives to the age of eighteen years in Consideration of which service the said Williams is to give her such Education, Clothing, Dyet [diet], Lodging as is by Law required. For the due performance of which the said Thomas Williams and Richard Haynie his Security acknowledged themselves bound to the Court now sitting in the sum of 5000$^£$ Tob^o. *OB 1773–83, 295.*

276. 14 July 1777—William Lowry orphan of William Lowry decd. is by the Court bound to Butler Williams untill [until] he arrives to the age of Twenty one years, in Consideration of which service the said Williams is to learn him the Trade of a Carpenter, and to give him such Education, Clothing, Diet and Lodging as is by Law required, for the due performance of which the said Butler Williams and George Edwards his Security acknowledged themselves bound

to the Court now sitting in the sum of 5000£ Tob°. *OB 1773–83, 297.*

277. 8 Sept. 1777—Catharine Wilkins orphan of John Wilkins deced is by the Court bound to James Oldham who together with William Kesterson his security entered into bond agreeable to Law the principal and the Security in 5000£ Tob°. The said orphan to be clothed & educated agreeable to Law. *OB 1773–83, 304.*

278. 8 Dec. 1777—Thomas Curtice orphan of George Curtice deced is by the Court bound to Isaac Rice till he arrives to the age of 21 years, the said Rice obliges himself to learn him the trade of a shoemaker and to read, write & cypher [cipher] as far as the rule of three for the performance of which he acknowledges himself bound to the Court in 5000 Pounds of Tob° & Norman Appleby agrees to become his security—the said orphan is to be clothed agreeable to Law. *OB 1773–83, 307.*

279. 9 March 1778—David Cottrel Orphan of Jn° Cottrel deced is by the Court bound to Peter Beane to learn the trade of a Taylor [tailor], to be clothed agreeable to Law and dieted and to read, write and Cypher [cipher] as far as the rule of three, for the performance of which the said Bean with George Bean his security acknowledged themselves bound to the Court the principal and ____ [no words in blank] the security in 5000£ Tob°. *OB 1773–83, 314.*

280. 13 April 1778—William Bailey Orphan of Daniel Bailey deced is by the Court bound to Peter Bean till he arrives to the age of 21 years to learn the Trade of a Taylor [tailor] & to read, write & cypher [cipher] as far as the rule of three for the due performance of which the said Bean with John Rogers his Security acknowledge themselves bound to the Court the principal—and the Security in 5000£ Tob°, the orphan to be dieted & clothed agreeable to Law. *OB 1773–83, 316.*

281. 14 April 1778—Rodham Thomas Orphan of Peter Thomas deced is by the Court bound to James Riveer till he arrives to the age of 21 Years to learn the Trade of a Silver Smith and to read, write and Cypher [cipher] as far as the rule of three for the performance of which the said Riveer with William Davenport his security acknowledge themselves bound to the Court in 5000£ Tob° the said Orphan to be dieted and cloathed [clothed] agreeable to Law. *OB 1773–83, 318.*

282. 14 April 1778—Rodham Tellus Orphan of John Tellus deced is by the Court bound to Thos Jones gent: till he arrives to the age of 21 years he being ____ [age not given in blank] years the ____ day of ____, he is to be learned the Trade of a Blacksmith, to read, write and cypher [cipher] as far as the rule of three for the performance of which the said Jones with James Knott his security acknowledges themselves bound to the Court the said Jones ____ & his Security in 5000£ Tob°, the said orphan to be clothed and dieted agreeable to Law. *OB 1773–83, 318.*

283. 14 April 1778—It is ordered that the Churchwardens of Saint Stephens Parish bind out Mary Bailey Orphan of Charles Bailey deced to George Rust agreeable to the Law in that case made & provided. *OB 1773–83, 320.*

284. 8 June 1778—It is ordered that the Churchwardens of Saint Stephens Parish bind out Mary Railey a bastard child of Sarah Railey according to Law. *OB 1773–83, 324.*

285. 8 June 1778—Thomas Walker Orphan of John Walker deced aged 16 years is by the Court bound to James Airs until he arrives to the age of 21 years. In consideration of which service the said James is to learn him the trade of a shoemaker and to give him such education, clothing, diet and lodging as is required by Law for the due performance of which the said James Airs and George Ball Junr his security acknowledge themselves bound to the Court now sitting in the sum of 5000$^£$ Tob^o. *OB 1773–83, 324.*

286. 8 June 1778—It is ordered that the Churchwardens of St Stephens Parish bind out Anne, Catherine, Churchill, and Mary Dunaway orphans of Joseph Dunaway deced according to Law. *OB 1773–83, 324.*

287. 15 Feb. 1774—Will of John Leach ... Item I give and bequeath to my son William Leach the other one half of my estate & for it to be sold in a convenient time after my decease by the Exors. and the money arising from the s^d sale to be kept by them while he arrives to eleven years of age and then for it to be bestowed on him in schooling and after he has got his schooling my will is that he should be bound to such a Trade as is approved by the Exors. ... *RB 9, Part 1, 324.*

288. 10 Aug. 1778—Daniel Palmer orphan of Nargill Sharezar Palmer Deced is by the Court bound to Richard Haynie untill [until] he arrives to the age of Twenty one years to learn the Trade of a Carpenter & Joiner for the performance of which the said Haynie with Ezekiel Hudnall his Security acknowledged themselves bound in Five thousand pounds of Tobacco. *OB 1773–83, 331.*

289. 14 Sept. 1778—On the motion of Eleanor Dyches to have her children set free from a former order of this Court made in November 1774 empowering the churchwardens of St Stephens Parish to bind them out & on hearing the evidence produced & the circumstances of the case, the Court are of opinion that the same be dismissed & the former order confirmed. [The spelling of the name in Document 263 is Dykes.] *OB 1773–83, 336.*

290. 12 Oct. 1778—Elizabeth Curtice orphan of George Curtice Deced is by the Court bound to Norman Appleby & Elizabeth his wife untill [until] she arrives to the age of Twenty one years for the performance of which the said Norman Appleby & Elizabeth his Bonds themselves in the sum of 5000$^£$ Tobacco & Isaac Rice Security. *OB 1773–83, 338.*

291. 12 July 1779—Ordered that the Church wardens of St Stephens Parish bind out John Drew an orphan to John Thomas according to Law. *OB 1773–83, 376.*

292. 12 July 1779—Ordered that the Church wardens of St Stephens parish bind out Boatman Drew an Orphan to Jesse Garner according to Law. *OB 1773–83, 377.*

293. 13 Sept. 1779—Ordered that the Churchwardens of St Stephens parish bind out Thomas Harcum a bastard child according to law. *OB 1773–83, 388.*

294. 8 Nov. 1779—John Drew Orphan of Richard Drew deced is by the Court bound to Richard Burton untill [until] he shall arrive to the age of Twenty one years to Learn the traid [trade] of a weaver whereupon he the said Richard Burton with William Burton his Security came into Court and acknowledged themselves bound in the Sum of 5000$^£$ of Tobacco for performance he the said John Drew being in his tenth year. *OB 1773–83, 394.*

295. 14 March 1780—Ordered that the Churchwardens of St Stephens Parish bind out Keziah Hudson orphan of Fielding Hudson deced. to William Clarke according to Law. *OB 1773–83, 404.*

296. 14 Aug. 1780—The complaint of Mary Hudson in behalf of her daughter Keziah Hudson against William Clarke is dismissed and It is ordered that the said Keziah return to her service. *OB 1773–83, 425.*

297. 8 Jan. 1781—Ordered that the Churchwardens of Wiccomoco [Wicomico] Parish bind out Charles and Thomas Brown Orphans of Thomas Brown deced according to Law. *OB 1773–83, 441.*

298. 14 May 1781—Ordered the Churchwardens of St Stephens parish Bind out Catherine, Elizabeth, Richard, and George Sebree children of William Sebree (who is a Soldier in the Continental Army) according to Law. *OB 1773–83, 460.*

299. 11 Jan. 1782—Ordered that the Churchwardens of St Stephens parish bind out Abishae Hudson according to Law. *OB 1773–83, 477.*

300. 11 Jan. 1782—Ordered that the Churchwardens of St Stephens Parish bind out Alice, Charles, Catesby and William Harford orphans of Mary Harford according to Law. *OB 1773–83, 477.*

301. 9 April 1782—Ordered that the Church Wardens of Wiccocomoco [Wicomico] parish bind out John Clarke orphan of _____ [(no name given)]

Clarke deced. according to Law. *OB 1773–83, 481.*

302. 10 Jan. 1783—John Way orphan of Richard Way Deced is by the Court bound to William Morton to learn the Trade of a Taylor [tailor], he the said Morton obliging himself to Comply with such requisites as the Law requires. Whereupon he together with Bridgar Haynie his Security acknowledged themselves bound in Two Thousand pounds of Tobacco for performance. *OB 1783–85, 3.*

303. 13 Jan. 1783—Vincent Garner son of Anne Garner is by the Court bound to William Morton to learn the Trade of a Taylor [tailor], he the said Morton obliging himself to Comply with such requisites as the Law requires. Whereupon he together with Bridgar Haynie his security acknowledged themselves bound in Two Thousands of Tob^o for performance. *OB 1783–85, 3.*

304. 13 April 1784—Ordered that the Churchwardens of St Stephens parish bind out Richard Edwards orphan of Thos Edwards deced. according to law. *OB 1783–85, 146.*

305. 10 May 1784—On the motion of Bennett Boush ordered that he be at liberty to assign over the Indenture which he hath for an orphan boy named Charles Lovelace Harford to Edwin Barns. *OB 1783–85, 158.*

306. 9 Aug. 1784—William Coleman orphan of Charles Coleman deced is by the Court Bound to John Almond untill [until] he attains the age of Twenty one years to learn the Trade of a Joiner. Whereupon the said John Almond with George Pickren his Security acknowledged themselves Severally bound for performance in the sum of 5000$^£$ Tob^o. *OB 1783–85, 226.*

307. 10 Aug. 1784—Charles Coleman orphan of Charles Coleman deced is by the Court bound to William Hughs untill [until] he arrives to the age of Twenty one years to Learn the Trade of a Taylor [tailor], the said Hughs obliges himself to find him sufficient Clothes, washing, Lodging & Diet. Whereupon he with Thomas Hobson his Security acknowledged themselves bound in 5000$^£$ Tob^o performance. *OB 1783–85, 232.*

308. 13 June 1785—Ordered that the Churchwardens of Wiccomoco [Wicomico] parish Bind out Charles Kent orphan of John Kent deced and also Nanny Hill orphan of John Hill deced according to Law. *OB 1783–85, 328.*

309. 8 Aug. 1785—John Way orphan of Richard Way deced is by the Court bound to Jordon Betts untill [until] he arrives to the age of twenty one years to learn the Trade of a Taylor [tailor], he the said Betts obliging himself to find him sufficient clothes, diet, etc. Whereupon he with Richard Way his security acknowledged themselves bound in 5000£ tobacco for performance. *OB 1783–85, 371.*

310.   10 Jan. 1786—Anthony Sydnor Routt is by the Court Bound to Richard Bennett untill [until] he attains the age of Twenty years to learn the traid [trade] of a Carpenter and Joiner and to find him good sufficient cloths [clothes] and accommodations, whereupon he together with Richard Routt his security acknowledged themselves Bound in the sum of 5000£ tobacco for performance. *OB 1786–90, Part 1, 6.*

311.   13 Feb. 1786—Ordered that the Churchwardens of St Stephens parish bind out Sally Popperwell to Elizabeth Oldham according to Law. *OB 1786–90, Part 1, 9.*

312.   13 Feb. 1786—Thomas Burton Orphan of Richard Burton deced is by the Court Bound to William Prosser to learn the traid [trade] of a House Carpenter and Joiner untill [until] he arrives to the age of Twenty One years and the said Prosser oblidging [obliging] himself to find Sufficient Clothes and Accomodations [accommodations] according to Law for the performance of which the said Prosser with William Clarke his Security acknowledged themselves bound to the Court in the Quantity of 5000£ Tobacco. *OB 1786–90, Part 1, 12.*

313.   13 Feb. 1786—Ewell Self Orphan of Henry Self deced is by the Court Bound to Richard Bennett to learn the traid [trade] of a House Carpenter and Joiner untill [until] he arrives to the age of Twenty one years the said Bennett oblidging [obliging] himself to find Sufficient Cloths [clothes] Accomodations [accommodations] according to law for the performance of which the said Bennett with John Middleton his Security acknowledged themselves Bound to the Court in the Quantity of 5000£ Tobacco. *OB 1786–90, Part 1, 13.*

314.   9 Oct. 1786—An Indenture of Apprenticeship from Abraham Dunaway to Thomas Thomas was proved by the Oaths of Thaddeus Williams George Glascock Junr and William McCarty Witnesses thereto and Ordered to be Recorded. *OB 1786–90, Part 1, 128.*

315.   9 Oct. 1786—This Indenture made this 21st day of September one Thousand Seven hundred and eighty six Between Abraham Dunaway of Northumberland County of the one part and Thomas Thomas of Richmond County of the other part Witnesseth that the said Abraham Dunaway hath bound and doth by these presents bind himself unto the above named Thomas Thomas of the afores^d County of Richmond for and during the term untill [until] he shall arrive to the age of twenty one years all which time of servitude he the said Abraham Dunaway shall behave himself as a faithfull [faithful] apprentice, his master's lawfull [lawful] commands obey and all his secrets

keep, never to abscon^d nor absent himself from his said master's Business day nor night unless leave first had or obtained, for which service the said Thomas Thomas doth oblige himself to find and provide for the said Abraham Dunaway during his servitude good and sufficient cloths [clothes], diet and lodging suitable for one of his capacity and to instruct him in the taylors [tailor's] Business as far as in his power lies. In Witness whereof the Parties to these presents have set their hands and seals the day and year first above written.

              his
          Abraham Dunaway
              mark
           Thos Thomas

RB 13, 250, 251.

316. 9 Oct. 1786—Ordered that the Overseers of the poor of St Stephens parish bind out Charles Ellicot, Sarah Popwell, William Dameron, Anne Dameron, John Dameron, Frances Dameron and Isaac Pickrell according to Law. *OB 1786–90, Part 1, 129.*

317. 9 Oct. 1786—Ordered that the overseers of the poor of St Stephens Bind out William Hawkins, Rodham France, James Harrison, Robert Gordon, Susanna Thomas and Jesse Richardson according to Law. *OB 1786–90, Part 1, 130.*

318. 8 Jan. 1787—On the motion of Winifred Walker Orphan of John Walker deced against Jane Humphries and Joseph Hudnall for the dues allowed by Law to Orphan apprentices. This day came the parties who being fully heard It is considered by the Court that the said Winifred Walker recover against the said Jane Humphries and Joseph Hudnall the Sum of Three pounds Ten Shillings for her dues aforesaid and her costs by her in this behalf Expended. *OB 1786–90, Part 1, 157.*

319. 12 Feb. 1787—Ordered that the Overseers of the Poor of St Stephens parish bind out Griffin Brin Orphan of Joshua Brin deced according to Law. *OB 1786–90, Part 1, 159.*

320. 11 June 1787—Upon the complaint of Abraham Dunaway against his Master Thomas Thomas for misusage, this day came the said parties who being fully heard, it is ordered that the said Abraham Dunaway be Discharged from all further Services as an apprentice to the said Thomas Thomas. *OB 1786–90, Part 1, 220.*

321. 9 July 1787—Ordered that Eli Mason orphan of Peter Mason dec^d be bound to William Prosser according to Law. *OB 1786–90, Part 1, 231.*

322. 10 Dec. 1787—Ordered that the Overseers of the poor of Wicco: [Wicomico] parish bind out the orphans of Enoch Potts dec^d according to Law.

OB 1786–90, Part 2, 304.

323. 15 April 1788—Ordered that the Overseers of the poor of this County bind out to George Beane, Grig Glascock Blackerby a poor orphan, according to Law. *OB 1786–90, Part 2, 345.*

324. 9 Dec. 1788—Ordered that the overseers of the poor in the upper district of St Stephens parish bind out Robert Black a poor orphan according to Law. *OB 1786–90, Part 2, 446.*

325. 9 Feb. 1789—Ordered that the overseers of the Poor in this County do bind out James Mason, Molly Curtice, Nancy Curtice, and Rachel Curtice Poor Orphans according to Law. *OB 1786–90, Part 2, 450.*

326. 14 April 1789—Ordered that the Overseers of the Poor do bind out Samuel Dameron to John Angel to learn the Trade or Occupation of a Blacksmith according to Law. *OB 1786–90, Part 2, 480.*

327. 14 April 1789—Ordered that the Overseers of the Poor do bind out John Wiggen to Roger W. Hughlett according to Law. *OB 1786–90, Part 2, 480.*

328. 13 July 1789—Ordered that the overseers of the poor in Wiccomoco [Wicomico] parish in this County bind out Thomas Turner and Thomas Rylie according to Law. *OB 1786–90, Part 2, 539.*

329. 14 Sept. 1789—Ordered that the Overseers of the Poor in the lower district of St Stephens Parish bind out Elisha Payne Hammertree according to Law. *OB 1786–90, Part 2, 566.*

330. 14 Sept. 1789—Ordered that the Overseers of the Poor in Wiccocomoco [Wicomico] Parish in this County bind out Richard Porter, John Dameron, Betty Porter, and Samuel Lunsford according to Law. *OB 1786–90, Part 2, 566.*

331. 12 Oct. 1789—Ordered that the Overseers of the Poor in the lower District of Saint Stephens Parish in this County do bind out Elisha Edwards, Daniel Edwards, William Edwards, and Ellen Edwards, Children of William Edwards; Elizabeth Betts Orphan of Betty Betts, and Betty Poplar Orphan of James Oldham according to Law. *OB 1786–90, Part 2, 568.*

332. 12 Oct. 1789—Ordered that the Overseers of the Poor in the lower district of Saint Stephens Parish in this County do bind out Betty Campbell daughter of Elizabeth Dawson Campbell to George Robinson according to Law. *OB 1786–90, Part 2, 569.*

333. 12 April 1790—Ordered that the overseers of the poor in the upper district of Saint Stephens parish do bind out John Neale according to Law. *OB*

1786–90, Part 2, 601.

334. 15 May 1790—Ordered that the Overseers of the Poor in the lower district of Saint Stephens Parish bind out Elizabeth Appleby Orphan of Norman Appleby decd and Orange Pickeren Orphan of John Pickeren decd according to Law. *OB 1786–90, Part 2, 615.*

335. 14 June 1790—Ordered that the overseers of the poor of Wiccocomoco [Wicomico] parish in this County do bind out Joseph Spriggs according to Law. *OB 1790–95, 2.*

336. 12 July 1790—Ordered that the overseers of the poor in the district of Wiccomoco [Wicomico] Parish bind out Thomas Gascock Blackerby according to Law. *OB 1790–95, 7.*

337. 13 Sept. 1790—Ordered that the overseers of the Poor in the lower district of Saint Stephen's Parish bind out John and Thomas Hogan Orphans of John Hogan deceased, and Rody Neale Orphan of Christopher Neale decd according to Law. *OB 1790–95, 33.*

338. 12 Oct. 1790—Ordered that the overseers of the poor of this County in the lower district of St Stephens parish do bind out James Garner, George Harcum, & David Piper according to Law. *OB 1790–95, 40.*

339. 13 June 1791—Ordered that the Overseers of the poor in the lower District of Saint Stephens Parish bind out Jane Bluford Orphan of Elijah Bluford deceased according to Law. *OB 1790–95, 136.*

340. 13 June 1791—Ordered that the Overseers of the Poor in the upper District of Saint Stephens Parish bind out Becky Brinn, Peggy Brinn, and Winny Brinn and Samuel French Orphans according to Law. *OB 1790–95, 138.*

341. 13 Sept. 1791—Ordered that the Overseers of the Poor in the lower District of Saint Stephens Parish bind out John, Thomas & William Bradger poor orphans according to Law. *OB 1790–95, 173.*

342. 10 July 1792—Ordered that John F. Fallin & Isaac Bayse gent. be appointed to bind Burgess Pitman to Fortunatus Pitman it appearing to the Court that the said Burgess has not sufficient estate to maintain him. *OB 1790–95, 245.*

343. 10 Sept. 1792—Ordered that John H. Fallin Gent. be appointed to bind George Waden Fletcher to Gideon Marsh according to Law. *OB 1790–95, 265.*

344. 8 Oct. 1792—Ordered that the Overseers of the Poor do bind out Joseph Spriggs Orphan of Joseph Spriggs deceased according to Law. *OB 1790–95, 268.*

345. 9 Oct. 1792—Ordered that the Overseers of the Poor bind Mary Ann Baylis Wilkins to Elizabeth Allsway according to Law. *OB 1790–95, 275.*

346. 14 Jan. 1793—Ordered that the overseers of the poor in the District of Wiccocomoco [Wicomico] Parish bind out George Waden Fletcher according to Law. *OB 1790–95, 297.*

347. 11 Feb. 1793—Ordered that the overseers of the poor in the lower District of Saint Stephens Parish do bind Samuel Moltimore & John Smither to learn the trade of a Taylor [tailor]. *OB 1790–95, 299.*

348. 10 June 1793 Ordered that the Overseers of the Poor in the lower District of Saint Stephens Parish do bind out Stewart Warren Thornton and Francis Hall according to Law. *OB 1790–95, 329.*

349. 14 Oct. 1793—Ordered that the Overseers of the Poor in the upper District of St Stephens Parish do bind out George Brown Orphan of Joseph Brown decd and Samuel Davis according to Law. *OB 1790–95, 362.*

350. 9 Dec. 1793—The Court do with the assent of Cynor Bell bind William son of the said Cynor to William Prosser until he arrives to the age of twenty one years to learn the trade of a Carpenter. *OB 1790–95, 377.*

351. 13 Jan. 1794—Ordered that the Overseers of the Poor in the District of Wiccocomoco [Wicomico] Parish bind out Lewis Sampson according to Law. *OB 1790–95, 381.*

352. 14 Oct. 1794—Ordered that the Overseers of the Poor in the upper District of Saint Stephens Parish bind out John Harris orphan of Jesse Harris deced according to Law. *OB 1790–95, 475.*

353. 8 June 1795—Ordered that the Overseers of the Poor in the lower District of Wiccocomoco [Wicomico] Parish bind out Thomas Turner Parker and Martin Hall according to Law and that their freedom dues be three pounds each. *OB 1790–95, 535.*

354. 14 Sept. 1795—Ordered that the Overseers of the Poor in the upper District in Saint Stephens Parish bind out Samuel Davis and William S. Thomas according to Law, and that they be allowed twelve Dollars each for their freedom dues respectively. *OB 1790–95, 562.*

355. 12 Oct. 1795—Ordered that the Overseers of the Poor in the lower District of St Stephens Parish bind out Shaderick Bee, James & Hacka Frobus, Champion and William Gill, Polly Redman, Sally Tignor, John & Betty Hopkins, Heli Pickren, William Trap, Greek Harcum, Robert Edwards, Stephen Corbell, and George Owens poor orphans according to Law. *OB 1790–95, 579.*

356. 14 Dec. 1795—Ordered that the Overseers of the Poor in the District of Wiccocomoco [Wicomico] Parish do bind out Dennis Swanson, Willis Swanson, William Swanson, Hezekiah Dameron, Jeremiah Dameron, and William Edwards Poor Orphans according to Law. *OB 1790–95, 597.*

357. 11 July 1796—Ordered that the Overseers of the Poor in the District of Wiccomico [Wicomico] Parish do bind out John Cessaty according to Law and that the Master of the said John Cessaty at the expiration of his apprenticeship pay him the sum of twenty dollars. *OB 1796–97, 33.*

358. 11 July 1796—Ordered that the Overseers of the poor in the district of Wiccomico [Wicomico] Parish do bind out James Adams according to law and that the master of the said James Adams at the expiration of his apprenticeship pay him the sum of ten dollars. *OB 1796–97, 34.*

359. 12 Sept. 1796—Ordered that the overseers of the poor in the lower district of Saint Stephens Parish do bind out John H. Popewell, Nancy Wagstaff, John Lowry, Sally Lowry, George Curtis, Peggy Lowry and Haynie Leland, poor orphans according to law. *OB 1796–97, 67.*

360. 12 Sept. 1796—Ordered that the overseers of the poor in the lower district of Saint Stephens Parish do bind out Hugh Owens, James Blueford, Samuel Jones, George Pickren, Rodham Bridgman and William Bridgman, idle boys, according to law. *OB 1796–97, 67.*

361. 14 Feb. 1797—Ordered that the overseers of the poor in the upper District of St Stephens Parish do bind out Ja^s Harison, Shapleigh France, John King & Wm King to Catesby Jones according to Law. *OB 1793–1800, 109.*

362. 14 Feb. 1797—Ordered that Wm Claughton gdn. [guardian] to Wm Routt do bind his s^d ward to Catesby Jones gent. clk [clerk] of the Court to learn the s^d occupation of clk. [clerk]. *OB 1793–1800, 109.*

363. 10 May 1797—Ord^d that the Overseers of the poor of the upper parish of St. Stephens bind Walter Shaw (a poor orphan) to Astin Hall according to Law. *OB 1793–1800, 119.*

364. 12 June 1797—Ord^d that the overseers of the poor of Wicc^o [Wicomico] parish bind Jeremiah & Hezekiah Dameron (poor orphans) to Jesse Chilton (of Lancaster County) according to law. *OB 1793–1800, 119.*

365. 9 July 1798—It appearing to the Court that Thomas Taylor to whom John Kessady, a poor orphan, was bound by order of this Court, has sold or turned him over to some other person without the assent of the Court & contrary to law. It is ord^d that the overseers of the poor of Wicco. [Wicomico] parish bind the said orphan to such other person as they may think proper till he arrives to the age of twenty one years. *OB 1793–1800, second half of book, 28.*

366. 10 July 1798—Ordered that the Overseers of the Poor of the lower District of St. Stephen's parish bind William Cornish (orphan of William Cornish) to Isaac Mott (Taylor) [tailor] according to law. *OB 1793–1800, second half of book, 35.*

367. 8 Oct. 1798—Ordered that the Overseers of the poor in the lower District of St Stephen's Parish bind Greek Harcum, a poor orphan to Isaac Mott (Taylor) [tailor] according to law. *OB 1793–1800, second half of book, 48.*

368. 8 April 1799—Ord^d that the Overseers of the poor of the lower district of St. Stephen's parish bind Hannah Humphris orphan of Geo. Humphris to Wm Wildy (Taylor) [tailor] according to law. *OB 1793–1800, second half of book, 68.*

369. 13 Jan. 1800—Ordered that the Overseers of the Poor in the lower District of St Stephens Parish bind out Sally, William & Samuel Lucas, orphans of Thomas Lucas decd. *OB 1793–1800, second half of book, 100.*

370. 13 Jan. 1800—Ordered that the Overseers of the Poor of the Upper District bind out Betty Mason daughter of Eli Mason according to law. *OB 1793–1800, second half of book, 100.*

371. 9 June 1800—Ord^d that the overseers of the poor in the upper district bind out a mulatto boy by the name of Daniel Ricks to Wm. Claughton according to law. *OB 1793–1800, second half of book, 131.*

372. 9 June 1800—Ord^d that the overseers of the poor in the upper district bind Betty Mason daughter of Eli Mason to Mary Elmore according to law. *OB 1793–1800, second half of book, 132.*

373. 8 Dec. 1800—Ord^d that James Kern be bound by the overseers of the poor to Henry Travers. *OB 1793–1800, second half of book, 170.*

374. 14 Sept. 1801—Ord^d that the overseers of the poor bind John Williams to Holland T. Dameron according to law. *OB 1801–07, 53.*

375. 12 July 1802—Ord^d that the overseers of the poor be appointed to bind Valentine Harcum to Isaac Carter according to law. *OB 1801–07, 112.*

376. 13 Sept. 1808—Order^d that the overseers of the poor bind out Danl Coats, a free mulatto boy, to John C. Straughan to learn the art of a house carpenter according to law. *OB 1807–11, 64.*

377. 11 Sept. 1809—Ord^d that the overseers of the poor of this County bind out Bill Thomas, son of Amey Thomas, a free mulatto, to Bridgar Haynie to learn the art of a cooper. *OB 1807–11, 124.*

378. 9 Oct. 1809—Ord^d that the overseers of the poor of this County bind Thomas Burk, a free mulatto boy, to John Grinsted to learn the trade of a carpenter. *OB 1807–11, 128.*

379. 8 Jan. 1810—Ord^d that the Overseers of the poor bind Betsy Hughlett to Spencer Thomas to learn the art of a weaver. *OB 1807–11, 149.*

380. 8 Jan. 1810—Ord^d that the overseers of the poor bind out Ellen Burk to John Lewis to learn the trade of a seamstress. *OB 1807–11, 149.*

381. 14 May 1810—Ord^d that the overseers of the poor of the upper district of St Stephens bind Griffin Jones, a free mulatto about 15 years of age, to John Maley to learn the art of a cooper—that they bind Adam, a free negro about 15 years of age, to Wm. Pierson to learn the art of a mariner—& that they bind Harriet, a mulatto girl about 11 years of age to Wm. Vanlandingham to learn the art of a spinner. *OB 1807–11, 176.*

382. 8 June 1812—Ord^d that the overseers of the poor bind John Thomas, son of Job Thomas, to Geo: Jones to learn the trade of a cooper. *OB 1811–15, 88.*

383. 14 June 1813—Ord^d that the overseers of the poor of upper St Stephens bind Cyrus Venie, a free negro boy, to Wm. Smither to learn the trade of a carpenter according to law. *OB 1811–15, 177.*

384. 14 Dec. 1813—Ord^d that the overseers of the poor of this County bind out Elijah (sometimes called Elijah Weaver), a free negro boy, to Ben: Lansdell jr. to learn the trade of a shoemaker. *OB 1811–15, 209.*

385. 9 May 1815—Ord^d that the overseers of the poor of Wicco: [Wicomico] bind out Armistead Jones, a free mulatto boy, to George Y. Bean to learn the trade of a wheelwright & carpenter. *OB 1811–15, 320.*

386. 11 Sept. 1815—Ord^d that the overseers of the poor bind Lavina Coats, a parishoner of St Stephens, to Ben: Turner to learn the business of a housewifery. *OB 1811–15, 373.*

387. 11 Sept. 1815—Ord^d that the overseers of the poor bind Armistead Jones, son of Hannah Jones, to Griffin Headley to learn the occupation of a farmer. *OB 1811–15, 373.*

388. 14 Oct. 1816—Ord^d that the overseers of the poor of upper St Stephens bind Vincent Brann, an orphan boy, to Ben: O. Smith to learn the trade of a baker. *OB 1816–20, 94.*

389. 9 June 1817—Ord^d that the overseers of the poor of Wicco: [Wicomico] bind Champion Carter & Wm. Toulson, orphan boys, until they arrive to 21 yrs. of age to George Groves to learn the trade of a cooper. *OB 1816–20, 152.*

390. 13 Oct. 1817—Ord^d that the overseers of the poor of Wicco: [Wicomico] bind Wm Snow & Frederick Mitchell, orphan boys of this county, to John Bryan to learn the trade of a cooper. *OB 1816–20, 188.*

391. 12 Jan. 1818—Ordered that the overseers of the poor of upper St Stephens bind out Thaddeus Wells, a free boy, to Wm. Rochester to learn the trade of a carpenter. *OB 1816–20, 214.*

392. 8 Feb. 1819—Ord^d that the overseers of the poor of U. [upper] St Stephens bind out William Day, a free boy of colour, to Elijah Moore to learn the trade of a carpenter. *OB 1816–20, 331.*

393. 13 Nov. 1820—Ord^d that the overseers of the poor of upper St. Stephens bind Orange Pickren to Tho. Jaques to learn the trade of a blacksmith. *OB 1820–25, 67.*

394. 11 Dec. 1820—Ord^d that the overseers of the poor of lower St Stephens bind James Carter, Hiram N. Yost & Joseph Wilson to Geo: Groves to learn the trade of a cooper. *OB 1820–25, 71.*

395. 9 Feb. 1829—Ord^d that the overseers of the poor of Wicco: [Wicomico] bind out Wm Dunaway, a poor orphan, to Hiram Yost to learn the trade of a cooper. *OB 1825–30, 334.*

396. 13 July 1829—Ord^d that the overseers of the poor of lower St Stephens bind out John Sank, a free boy of colour, to Peter Adams to learn the trade of a carpenter. *OB 1825–30, 372.*

397. 12 July 1830—Ordered that the overseers of the poor of Wicco: [Wicomico] bind Wm Ashburn, orphan of Haynie Ashburn dec^d, to Hiram Ingram to learn the art of a mariner and that the overseers of upper St. Stephens bind Joseph Jones, son of Winney Jones, to Wm Rice to learn the trade of a shoe maker. *OB 1825–30, 462.* [Wrong page listed in index of Order Book.]

398. 14 June 1831—Ord^d that the overseers of poor of Wicco: [Wicomico] parish bind Richd Moore orphan of Charles Moore dec^d to Luke Ball to learn the trade of boot & shoe maker. *OB 1830–35, 96.*

399. 9 Jan. 1832—On the motion of Hiram Davis Gdn. [guardian] to Geo: Pickering his ward, above the age of 16 years, It is ord^d that it be entered of record that the s^d gdn hath the approbation of this court to bind the said George by & with the consent of him the s^d George an apprentice to James M. Smith to learn the art or trade of Tanning & currying till the said Geo: Pickering shall attain 22 years of age which will be on the 1st day of January 1836. *OB 1830–35, 126.*

400. 9 Jan. 1832—This Indenture made and entered into this 9th day of January 1832 between Hiram Davis Guardian to George Pickering & the said George Pickering of the County of Northumberland of the one part & James M. Smith of the said County of the other part. Witnesseth that the said George Pickering voluntarily, & with the consent of the said Hiram Davis his Guardian & by & with the approbation of the court of the county aforesaid hath put, placed & bound himself & by these presents doth put place and bind himself to be an apprentice with him the said James M. Smith & apprentice with him the said James M. Smith to dwell till the said George Pickering shall attain the age of twenty two years, which will be on the first day of January 1836, during all which term the said Hiram Davis & the said George Pickering do covenant and agree to and with the said James M. Smith that the said George Pickering the said James M. Smith shall will and truly serve in all such lawful business that the said George Pickering shall be put unto by his said master according to the best of his power, wit, & ability of him the said George Pickering & honestly & obediently shall behave himself towards the said James M. Smith, & honestly & obediently unto the Family of the said James M. Smith and the said James M. Smith, on his part doth covenant and agree to & with the said George Pickering that he the said James M. Smith will and truly instruct (or cause to be instructed) in the art or trade of Tanning & Currying & will use all due diligence to make the said George Pickering as perfect on the said art or trade of Tanning & Currying as possible and that the said James M. Smith will allow unto the said George Pickering good & sufficient, meat, drink, apparel, washing, lodging, and all other things suitable for an apprentice during the said term. In witness whereof the parties to these presents have hereunto set their hands & affixed their seals the day and year first above written.

in the presence of
    Saml. Blackwell
RB 27, 4, 5.

Hiram Davis
Geo: Pickering
J.M. Smith

401. 11 June 1832—Ord[d] that the overseers of the poor for upper St Stephens bind out the following mulatto orphan children to be respectively taught trades to wit: Wm Cornish, Juliet Cornish, and Elizabeth Hall. *OB 1830–35, 177.*

402. 14 Aug. 1832—Ord[d] that the overseers of the poor of upper St Stephens bind out Hiram Cornish to be taught a trade. *OB 1830–35, 200.*

403. 8 Oct. 1832—Indenture of apprenticeship from o.p. [overseers of the poor] to Frances Rock. *OB 1830–35, 210.*

404. 8 Oct. 1832—This Indenture made this the eight day of October in the year of our Lord one thousand eight hundred and thirty two between Thomas Bell, Richard Headley and Thomas G. Rains overseers of the poor for upper St. Stephens district in the county of Northumberland of the one part, and Frances Rock, of the said county of the other part, Witnesseth, that the said Thomas Bell, Richard Headley and Thomas G. Rains overseers of the poor as aforesaid, by virtue of an order of the Court of the aforesaid county, bearing date June Term one thousand eight hundred thirty two, have put placed and bound, and by these presents as put place and bind William Cornish a mulatto orphan of the age of five years, to be an apprentice with him the said Frances Rock to dwell from the date of these presents untill [until] the said William Cornish shall come to the age of twenty one years according to the act of the general assembly in that case made and provided. By and during all of which time and term the said William Cornish shall the said Frances Rock his s^d master will and faithfully serve in all such lawfull business as the said William Cornish shall be put unto by his said master according to the power wit and ability of him the said William Cornish and honestly & obediently in all things shall behave himself towards his said master and honestly and orderly towards the rest of the family of the said Frances Rock, And the said Frances Rock for his part, for himself, his executors and administrators doth hereby promise and covenant to and with the s^d overseers of the poor and every of them, their and every of their executors, and administrators, and their and every of their successors for the time being, & to and with the said William Cornish that the said Frances Rock shall the said William Cornish that the said Frances Rock shall the said William Cornish in the craft and mistery [mystery] and occupation of a blacksmith which the said Frances Rock now useth, after the best manner, that he can or may teach, instruct and inform or cause to taught instructed and informed, as much as thereunto belongeth or in any wise appertaineth, and that the said Frances Rock shall also find and allow unto the said apprentice sufficient meat, drink, apparel, washing, lodging, and all other things needfull or meet for an apprentice during the term aforesaid: And will moreover pay to the said William Cornish the sum of twelve dollars at the expiration of the said term. In witness whereof the parties to these presents have interchangeably set their hands & seals the day and year first above written.

            Thomas Bell
            Richd Headley
            Thomas Rock

At a court held for Northumberland County at the courthouse on Monday the 8th of October 1832. This Indenture was acknowledged by the parties thereto, and ordered to be recorded.

          teste
            W.B. Cralle C.C.

RB 27, 180, 181.

405. 8 Oct. 1832—This Indenture made this the day in the year of our Lord one thousand eight hundred and thirty two, between Thos Bell, Richard Headley, & Thos G. Rains overseers of the poor for upper St. Stephens district in the County of Northumberland of the one part, and Alexander Rock of the said County and State of the other part; Witnesseth, that the said Thomas Bell, Richard Headley and Thomas G. Rains overseers of the poor as aforesaid, by virtue of an order of the Court of the aforesaid County bearing date June ten in the year one thousand and eight hundred and thirty two have put, placed and bound and by these presents do put place and bind Eliz^a Hall a mulatto orphan aged about four years to be an apprentice with him the Alexander Rock to dwell from the date of these presents untill [until] the said Eliz^a Hall shall come to the age of eighteen years, according to the act of the General Assembly in that case made and provided—By and during all of which time and term, the said Alexander Rock, her said master will and faithfully serve in all such lawfull [lawful] business as the said Eliz^a Hall shall be put unto by her said master, according to the power wit, and ability of her the said Eliz^a Hall, and honestly and obediently in all things shall behave herself towards her said master, and honestly and orderly towards the rest of the family of the said Alexander Rock—and the said Alexander Rock for his part, for himself, his executors, and administrators doth hereby promise and covenant with the said overseers of the poor, and every of their and every of their executors and admins: their and every of their successors for the time being and to and with the said Eliz^a Hall, that he the said Alexander Rock shall the said Eliz^a Hall in the craft, mistery [mystery] and occupation of a spinner which is now used by the wife of the said Alexander Rock, after the best manner, that can or may have her taught, instructed and informed, as much as thereunto belongeth or in any wise appertained—And the said Alexander Rock shall also find and allow unto the said apprentice, sufficient meat drink and apparell [apparel], washing, lodging and all other things needfull and meet for an appprentice during the term aforesaid—And will more over pay to the said Eliz^a Hall the sum of twelve dollars at the expiration of the aforesaid term. In witness whereof the parties to these present have interchangeably set their hands and affixed their seals the day and year above written.

Thos Bell
Richd Headley
Alexander Rock

At the court held for Northumberland County at the court house on Monday the 8th of October 1832—This deed was acknowledged by the parties thereto and ordered to be recorded. *RB 27, 181, 182.*

406. 8 Oct. 1832—This Indenture made this the eight day of October in the year of our Lord one thousand and eight hundred and thirty two between Thomas Bell, Richard Headley & Thomas G. Rains Overseers of the poor of upper St. Stephens district in the county of Northumberland of the one part and William Rock of the said county of the other part-Witnesseth, that the said Thomas Bell, Richard Headley, and Thomas G. Rains overseers of the poor as aforesaid by virtue of an order of the Court of the aforesaid county bearing date the fourteenth day of August in the year one thousand eight hundred and thirty two; have put placed and bound, and by these presents do put place and bind

Hiram Cornish a mulatto orphan aged about twelve years to be an apprentice with him the said William Rock to dwell from the date of these presents untill [until] the said Hiram Cornish shall come to the age of twenty one years according to the act of the General Assembly in that case made and provided; By and during all of which time and term the said Hiram Cornish shall the said William Rock his said master will & faithfully serve in all such lawfull [lawful] business as the said Hiram Cornish shall be put unto by his master, according to the power wit and ability of him the said Hiram Cornish, and honestly and obediently in all things shall behave himself towards his said master, and honestly and obediently to the rest of the family of the said William Rock- And the said William Rock for his part for himself his executors and admors: [administrators] doth hereby promise covenant to an [and] with the said overseers of the poor, and every of them, their and every of their exors and admors their and every of their successors for the time being and to and with the said Hiram Cornish, that he the said William Rock shall the said Hiram Cornish in the Craft mystery and occupation of a blacksmith which is now used by the said William Rock after the best manner that he can or may have him taught instructed and informed as much as these unto belongeth in any wise appertaineth- And the said William Rock shall also find and allow unto the said apprentice sufficient meat, drink, and apparel washing lodging and all other things needfull [needful] and meet for an apprentice during the term aforesaid- And will more over pay to the said Hiram Cornish the sum of twelve dollars at the expiration of the aforesaid term-In witness whereof the parties to these presents have interchangeability set their hands & affixed their seals the day and year aforesaid.

Thomas Bell
Richd Headley
William Rock

At a court held for Northumberland County at the courthouse on Monday the 8th of October 1832. This deed was acknowledged by the parties thereto, and ordered to be recorded.

Teste
W.B. Cralle C.C.

RB 27, 182, 183.

407. 12 Nov. 1832—Indenture of apprenticeship from overseers of the poor to Jno. Patton acknowledged & o.k. *OB 1830–35, 213.*

408. 12 Nov. 1832—This Indenture made this 5th day of November in the year of our Lord one thousand eight hundred and thirty two between Thomas Bell, Richard Headley & Thomas G. Rains overseers of the poor of upper St Stephens district in the county of Northumberland of the one part, and John Patten of the said county of the other part Witnesseth. That the said Thomas Bell, Richard Headley & Thomas G. Rains, overseers of the poor as aforesaid, by virtue of an order of the court of the aforesaid county bearing date June ten in the year one thousand eight hundred and thirty two, have put, placed and bound, and by these presents do put, place and bind Juliet Cornish a mulatto orphan aged about eleven years old to be an apprentice with him the said John Patten to dwell from the date of these presents untill [until] the said Juliet Cornish shall come to the age of eighteen years according to the act of the General Assembly in the case made and provided. By and during all which time and term the said Juliet Cornish, shall the said John Patten her said master well and faithfully serve in all such lawfull [lawful] business as the said Juliet Cornish shall be put unto her said master, according to the power, wit and ability of her the said Juliet Cornish and honestly and obediently in all things shall behave herself towards her said master, and honestly and orderly towards the rest of the family of the said John Patten—And the said John Patten for his part, for himself, his executors and administrators, doth hereby promise and covenant to & with the said overseers of the poor and every of them, their and every of their executors, and administrators, their and every of their successors for the time being, and to and with the said Juliet Cornish, that he the said John Patten, shall the said Juliet Cornish, in the craft, mystery and occupation of a spiner [spinner] which is now used by the wife of the said John Patten, after the best manner that he can or may have her taught, instructed and informed as much as thereunto, belongeth or in any wise appertaineth—And that the said John Patten shall also find and allow unto the said apprentice sufficient meat, drink and apparel, washing, lodging and all the other things needfull [needful] and meet for an apprentice during the term aforesaid—And will moreover pay to the said Juliet Cornish the sum of twelve dollars at the expiration of the aforesaid Term—In witness whereof the parties to these presents have interchangeably set their hands & affixed their seals the day and year above written.

           Tho: Bell
           Richd Headley
           John Patten

RB 27, 198, 199.

409. 11 Feb. 1833—Forrester to Lackey Indenture of apprenticeship acknowledged & O.K. *OB 1830–35, 238.*

410. 11 Feb. 1833—This Indenture made & entered in this _____ [no date entered] day of 1833 between William W. Forester parent to Rich'd P. Forester and the s^d Richard P. Forester of the County of North'd of the one part & John T. Lackey of the sd. County of the other part Witnesseth that the said Richard P. Forester volentarly [voluntarily] & with the consent of the sd. William W. Forester his father & by & with the approbation of the Court of this County afsd. hath put, placed & bound himself & by these presents doth put, place & bind himself to be an apprentice with him the sd John T. Lackey & as an apprentice with him the sd John T. Lackey to dwell till the s^d Rich'd Forester shall attain to the age of twenty one years which will be in Oct. 1839 dureing [during] all which term the s^d William Forester & the s^d Richard Forester do covenant & agree to & with the s^d John Lackey that the s^d Richard P. Forester the s^d John T. Lackey shall well & truly serve in all such lawful business as the s^d Rich'd

Forester shall be put at by his s^d master according to the best of his power, wit & ability of him the s^d Rich'd Forester & honestly & obediently shall behave himself towards the sd John T. Lackey & honestly & obediently towards the family of the s^d Lackey & the s^d John T. Lackey on his part doth covenant & agree to & with the s^d Rich'd P. Forester that he the s^d John T. Lackey will well & truly instruct or cause to be instructed the s^d Richard P. Forester in the art & trade of carriage making to wit, to do all the wood work about carriages, coaches, gigs, etc. & will use all diligence to make the s^d Richard P. Forester as perfect in the s^d art or trade of carriage making as possible & that the s^d John T. Lackey will allow unto the s^d Rich'd P. Forester good & sufficient meat & drink, apparell [apparel], washing, lodging & all other things suitable for an apprentice dureing [during] the s^d time. In witness whereof the s^d parties to these presents have hereunto set their hands & affixed their seals the day & year first above written signed sealed & delivered.

          Wm W. Forester
          Richard P. Forester
          John T. Lackey

RB 27, 271, 272.

411. 10 March 1834—Ord^d that the overseers of Wicco: [Wicomico] bind Bald. Nicken to Tho. Rock to be taught the trade of a house carpenter. *OB 1830–35, 346.*

412. 11 Jan. 1836—An Indenture of apprenticeship between Eliz. Burress, Wm W. Burress & Isaac Haynie ack^d [acknowledged] & O.K. *OB 1835–44, 2.*

413. 11 Jan. 1836—This Indenture made this 11th day of January in the year of 1836 Between Betsy Burress & Wm Burress her son of the County of Northumb^d of the one part & Isaac Haynie of the s^d county of the other part witnesseth that the s^d William Burress volinturely [voluntarily] & with the approbation of the s^d Betsy hath placed and bound himself and by these presence doth part, place and bind himself William Burress to be an apprentice with him the s^d Haynie and as an apprentice with him the s^d Haynie to dwell till the s^d Wm Burress shall attain the age of Twenty one years which will be on the 1st day of August in the year 1849 during all which time the s^d Betsy & Wm Burress do covenant and agree to and with the s^d Haynie that the s^d Wm Burress shall well and faithfully serve in all such lawful business as the s^d Wm Burress shall be put unto by the s^d Master according to the best of power, wit and ability of the s^d Burress and honestly and obediently shall behave himself towards the said Haynie and honestly and orderly towards the family of the s^d Haynie and the s^d Haynie on his part doth covenant and agree to and with the s^d Wm Burress that the s^d Isaac Haynie will well and truly Instruct the said Burress in the art or mystery of a farmer which the s^d Haynie now followeth and will ____ [word not readable] all due diligence to make the s^d Burress as perfect in the s^d art or mystery of a farmer as possible and that the s^d Haynie will allow to the s^d Burress good and sufficient meat, drink, appeerel [apparel], washing, lodging and all other things suitable for an apprentice during the s^d time. In witness whereof the parties to these presence have hereunto set their hands and affixed their seals the day and year first above written.

             her
           Elizabeth Burress
             mark
             his
       William W.   Burress
             mark
          Isaac Haynie

RB 29, 9, 10.

414. 14 Jan. 1839—John Sank, who was bound by the overseers of the poor under an order of the court to Peter Adams to learn the trade of house carpenter, came into court and by the consent of the s^d Peter Adams & for reasons appearing to the court, it is ordered that the said order & the proceedings had under it be rescended [rescinded], & it is ord^d that the s^d Jno. Sank be by the overseers of the poor of lower St Stephens parish be bound to Lucius S. Winstead to learn the trade of a blacksmith. *OB 1835–44, 158.*

415. 9 Jan. 1843—Ord^d that the overseers of the poor of this county bind James Harcum to Jno. Lackey to learn the trade of a carriage maker. *OB 1835–44, 345.*

416. 10 April 1843—Ord^d that overseers of the poor for upper St. Stephens parish bind out Thaddeus King to Wm Rock to be taught the blacksmith trade & Wm Davy King to Edward Ashburn to be taught the trade of a house carpenter. *OB 1835–44, 357.*

417. 8 May 1843—Ord^d that the overseers of the poor for upper St Stephens bind Jos. Vanlandingham, a colored lad, to John H. Elmore to learn the trade of a farmer. *OB 1835–44, 359.*

418. 10 June 1844—Ord^d that the overseers of the poor in this county bind James Carter to Robert Sullivant to learn the trade of a carpenter. *OB 1844–52, 7.*

419. 1 Jan. 1846— ... Robert Alexander, James Haynie and Thomas L. Lyell, overseers of the poor, as aforesaid, by virtue of an order of the Court of the aforesaid County, bearing date the ninth day of December 1845, have put, placed and bound, and by these presents, do put, place and bind Wm Barker of the age of fifteen years (the 22nd day of February 1845) to be an apprentice with him the said James A. Snead, and as an apprentice with him the said James A. Snead to dwell from the date of these presents until the said Wm Barker shall attain the age of twenty one years (which will be the 22nd February 1851) according to the act of the general assembly in that case made and provided. By and during all which time and term the said Wm Barker shall the said James A. Snead, his said master, well and faithfully serve, in all such lawful business as the said Wm Barker shall be put unto by his said master, according to the powers, wit, and ability of him, the said Wm Barker, and honestly and obediently in all things shall behave himself towards his said master, and honestly and orderly towards the rest of the family of the said James A. Snead. And the sd James A. Snead for his part for himself, his executors, and administrators doth hereby promise and covenant to and with the overseers of the poor, and every of them, their and every of their executors and administrators and their and every of their successors for the time being and to and with them the said Wm Barker, that he the said James A. Snead shall instruct the said Wm Barker in the craft, mystery and occupation of a harness maker, which he the said James A. Snead now uses after the best manner that he can or may teach, instruct and inform or cause to be taught, instructed or informed as much as there unto belongeth, or in any wise appertaineth, and that the said James A. Snead shall also find and allow unto the said apprentice sufficient meat, drink, apparel, washing, lodging and all other things needful or meet for an apprentice during the term aforesaid and also that the said James A. Snead shall teach or cause to be taught to the said Wm Barker reading, writing, and common arithmetic, and will moreover pay the said Barker the sum of twelve dollars at the expiration of the aforesaid term. In witness whereof the parties have interchangeable set their hands and seals to these presents the day and year first above written.

                                         Robert Alexander
                                         James Haynie
                                         James A. Snead

RB 34, 350.

420. 1 Jan. 1846—Cyrus Harding and Charles L. Brown, overseers of the poor for the parish of Wicomico, bind Wm Greenwood (age fourteen the first day of July 1845) an apprentice to James A. Snead to learn the occupation of a saddler. James A. Snead is also to teach or cause to be taught Wm Greenwood reading, writing, and common arithmetic and pay him twelve dollars at the expiration of the term. [This indenture is very lengthy and worded very similar to the preceding one.] RB 34, 351.

421. 10 Aug. 1846—This Indenture made this 10th day of August in the year of our Lord 1846, between Cyrus Harding, Charles L. Brown and Wm H. Harding, overseers of the poor for Wiccomico [Wicomico] parish in the County of Northumberland of the one part, and James Martin of the said County of the other part, Witnesseth that the said Cyrus Harding, Charles L. Brown & Wm H. Harding, overseers of the poor as aforesaid, by virtue of an order the County Court of North^d bearing the 8th day of June 1846, have put, placed & bound, and by these presents do put, place & bind Frances Keiser of the age of 8 years and Frederick Keiser of the age of 4 years, children of Polly Keiser, and Emily Nicken of the age of 6 years and Wm Nicken of the age of 3 years, orphans of

Betsey Nickens dec^d to be apprentices with him the said James Martin, and as apprentices with him the said James Martin to dwell from the date of these presents until the said male children shall come to the years of twenty one years and the female children shall come to the age of eighteen according to the act of the General Assembly in that case made and provided. By and during all which time and term, the said Frances Keiser, Ferdinand Keiser, Emily Nicken and William Nicken, shall the said James Martin their said master, well and faithfully serve in all such lawful business as the said Frances Keiser, Ferdinand Keiser, Emily Nicken and Wm Nicken shall be put unto by their said master according to the power, wit and ability of them the said Frances Keiser, Ferdinand Keiser, Emily Nicken and William Nicken and honestly and obediently in all things shall behave themselves toward their said master James Martin, and honestly and orderly towards the rest of the family of the said James Martin. And the said James Martin for his part, for himself, his executors and administrators doth hereby promise and covenant to and with the said overseers of the poor, and every of them and every of their executors & administrators and their and every of their successors for the time being and to and with the sd. Frances Keiser, Ferdinand Keiser, Emily Nicken and William Nicken, that he the said James Martin shall _____ [space left blank; obviously it should be teach] said male children in the craft, mystery and occupation of a farmer or planter which the said James Martin now useth and the said female children in the craft, mystery and occupations of a weaver and spinner which the wife of the said James Martin now useth after the best manner that he can or may teach, instruct and inform or cause to be taught, instructed and informed as much as thereunto belongeth or in any wise appertaineth and that the said James Martin shall also find and allow unto the said apprentices sufficient meat, drink, apparel, washing, lodging and all other things needful and meet [fitting, useful, proper] for apprentices during the term aforesaid, and will moreover pay unto the said apprentices the sum of twelve dollars each at the expiration of their said terms. In witness whereof the parties to these presents have interchangeably set their hands and seals the day and year above written. [In one instance the name is Frederick Keiser; in all other cases it is Ferdinand.] *RB 34, 436.*

422. 12 June 1848—Ordered that the overseers of the poor bind out the orphans of Brenet Watkins. *OB 1844–52, 207.*

423. 13 May 1850—Ordered that the overseers of the poor of this county bind out the following indigent free negro children to Charles B. Turner to wit: William Thompson, age 12 years, to be a sailor; John Thompson, age 10, to be a farmer; and Osbern Thompson, 8 years of age, to be a farmer. The aforesaid boys are all children of Sophia Thompson, a free negro. After each of said children arrives at the age of 15 years, the said Turner shall pay their mother the sum of $10 annually for each until they arrive at the age of 21. *OB 1844–52, 336.*

424. 11 Aug. 1851—Ordered that the overseers of the poor of this County bind out to John Cookman the following indigent free negro girl Amanda, age three years, to learn the trade of sewing & weaving, until she attains the age of eighteen years. *OB 1844–52, 425.*

425. 12 April 1852—Ordered that the overseers of poor bind out to R.H. Jones, a free negro boy, Thurston Thomas, son of Harriet Thomas, age six years old, to learn the art of a dining room servant until he attains the age of twenty one. *OB 1844–52, 463.*

Court Records of Apprenticeships Overlooked in Compiling
Northumberland County, Virginia, Apprenticeships 1650–1750

426. 20 May 1650—This Indenture Witnesseth that John Corbill sonn [son] to John Corbill late of London, cleargyman [clergyman] deceased hath put him selfe [self] apprentice to Edward Cole of   in Virginia planter with him to dwell and serve for and dureinge [during] the tyme [time] and space of thirteen years fully to be compleat [completed] and ended to commence and beginn [begin] from the five and twenty day of November last untill [until] the said thirteen yeares [years] shall be fully expired dureinge [during] ... terme the said Apprentice shall doe [do] all such services and imployments [employments] as his said Master shall command and appoynt [appoint] and it is hereby ... and agreed upon between the said parties that the said Edward Coles nor his wife there [their] Executors or Administrators shall not bound out his said Apprentice to any other person whatsoever and the said Apprentice is to be free att [at] the death of the longest liver of the said Edward Coles or his wife and the said Edward Coles doth hereby bind himselfe [himself] his Executors and Administrators to give and deliver unto the said Apprentice att [at] the end of the said first twelfe [twelve] years one Cow with Calfe [calf] and att [at] the end of his tyme [time] one Sow with piggs [pigs], one gunn [gun], one pott [pot], one fryinge [frying] pann [pan] and axe, one hoe, one flockbead bolster and rugge [rug] together with double apparell [apparel] and three barrills [barrels] of Corne [corn] and to the true performance hereof the partyes [parties] above said doe [do] bind themselves each to other firmly by these presents. In wittness [witness] whereof the parties above said interchangably have put there [their] hands and seales [seals] the 20th day of May 1650.

Signum
John Corberill

Deeds Orders 1650–52, 39.

427. 4 Feb. 1651—Will of Jane Perie/Pery ... son Andrew shall be bound Apprentice to Hugh Lee for eight yeares [years] to teach him to reade [read] & write and to give him at the end of the time two suites [suits] of apparrel [apparel] and a cow calfe [calf]. *RB 1652–58, 7.*

428. 26 Nov. 1652—This Indenture made the 26th day of Novem: ... Betweene [between] Walter Weekes of Cherry point in the County of Northumberland & Colony of Virginia on the one part and Wm Allenson of the same place on the other part Witnesseth that the said Wm Allenson hath putt [put] out Walter Allenson his sone [son] an apprentice unto the said Walter

Weekes & with him after the maner [manner] of an Apprentice to serve & dwell from the day of the date hereof untill [until] . . . [page worn] full end & terme [term] of fifteene [fifteen] yeares [years] from hereto forth ensueing [ensuing] be fully compleated [completed] & ended Dureing [during] all wch terme [term] the said Apprentice his said master shall faithfully serve in such imploym^t [employment] as his said master shall imploy [employ] him in & put him to according to his best endeavour & power. In consideration whereof the said Walter Weekes doth promise, covenant & grant to & with the said Walter Allenson to provide, finde [find], allowe [allow] & give unto his said Apprentice dureing [during] all the tearme [term] aforesaid sufficient meat, drinke [drink], apparrell [apparel], lodging, washing & all other necessaries fitt [fit] & meate [meet: adj; early use of word meaning fitting, suitable, proper] for him to have & weare [wear] and likewise the said Walter Weekes doth promise to teach the said Apprentice to read English soe [so] soone [soon] as he shalbe [shall be] capable of teaching and also with two yeares [years] after the date hereof will give unto the said Walter Allenson his Apprentice a cow calfe [calf] and all the increase female that shall come & fall thereof dureing [during] the time of his Apprenticeship alwayes [always] provided that if the said Apprentice shall happen to dye [die] before the terme [term] of yeares [years] aforesaid be compleated [completed] & served then the said cow calfe [calf] & all her increase female shall revert and returne [return] unto the said Walter Weekes any promise, grant, gift herein granted, promised & given to the contrary in any wise not withstanding. In witness whereof the said Walter Weekes & Wm Allenson to this Indenture have set their hands & seales [seals] the day & year above written. Walter Weekes Signum. Wm Allenson Signed & Sealed in the presence of Signum John Kent, Tho Wilsford. Recorded this Indenture the 27th Novem: 1652. *RB 1652–58, 14.*

429. 10 March 1656—Will of William Walker . . . I doe [do] give my Eldest Sonne [son] John Walker unto my Friend Wm Colman for the tearme [term] of seaven [seven] yeares [years] my Sonne [son] to be at his own dispose to chuse [choose] where hee [he] will be guided; p:vided [provided] that the s^d Wm Colman shall find & p:vide [provide] for him sufficient meate [meat], drinke [drink], washing, lodgeing [lodging] & to teach him for to reade [read] p:fect [perfect] English in the tearme [term] aforesd & if the s^d Wm Colman doe [do] dye [die] during the s^d tearme [term] then my Sonne [son] to be at his own dispose. *RB 1652–58, 108.*

430. 20 Feb. 1659—Will of Sampson Cooper . . . Allsoe [also] . . . sonne [son] Samuel shall . . . be sent for England this next & every with him all such sumes [sums] of . . . received, and when hee [he] my son . . . that then hee [he] bind himselfe [himself] an Apprentice . . . Cocke Silbeman at the Signe [sign] of . . . Poultry at London. [Entire Indenture in very poor condition.] *RB 1658–66, 33.*

431. 11 March 1660—Certify all whome [whom] it may concerne [concern] y^t I Richard White doe [do] Indent with John Bearman that my Daughter . . . [page worn] White shall serve the s^d John Bearman after the ... [page worn] hereof the full terme [term] of nine yeares [years] in wch time the s^d Jno Bearman shall be engaged that his wife shall teach her to doe [do] all sort of worke [work] that shee [she] her selfe [self] can doe [do], that it is to say soweing [sewing], to learne [learn] her to reade [read]. The Condition of this Indenture is such that what stock I shall give into the hands of the s^d Jno Bearman for the use of my Daughter Hannah White of the increase hee [he] shall have the males & my Daughter the females. In Testimony hereof I sett [set] my hand the 11th day of March 1660.

Witness: Rich: Sutton the mark of John Bearman
    Rich: Rayman Rich: White his mark

RB 1658–66, 107.

432. 6 Nov. 1661—This Agreem^t [agreement] made ye 6th of Nov. between John Gibson of one pty: [party] & John Place on ye other pty [party] witnesseth y^t sd Jno Place do covenant & agree to serve & abide wth ye sd Jno Gibson for ye space of [page worn] yeares [years] after ye date hereof to be imployed [employed] in all manner [page worn] full service y^t ye sd Gibson shall imploy [employ] him in duringe [during] ye terme [term] of three yeares [years], beating at ye master excepted unless ye sd [page worn] doe [do] likewise beat himselfe [himself] in consideration whereof ye sd Gibson doth hereby engage himselfe [himself] to teach ye sd Place all y^t [page worn] selfe [self] in the Carpenters Trade not concealing any thing y^t he is willinge [willing] to learne [learn] & to allow unto ye sd [page worn] good dyet [diet], washing & lodging wth three thousand [page worn] merchantable tobacco & caske [cask], y^t is to say five hundred pounds ye first year, one thousand ye second year, [page worn] ye third year & y^t both parties are hereto agreed [page worn] sett [set] their hands & seale [seal] ye day & yeare [year] above written wth this p:mise y^t ye sd Gibson shall pay levy.

              John Place
              John Gibson

RB 1658–66, 175.

Index

Names of apprentices, their parent or parents when given, and persons to whom they have been apprenticed have been indexed according to document number. Names of apprentices appear in italics.

Abby
   John 242
Adams
   James 358
   Peter 396, 414
Airs
   James 285
   William 69, 70
   William 70
Alexander
   John 174
   John Shildon 174
Allenson
   Walter 428
   William 428
Allsway
   Elizabeth 345
Almond
   John 306
Alverson
   Richard 12
Anderson
   Andrew 107, 108
   William 33, 34
Angel
   John 326
Appleby
   Elizabeth 334
   Elizabeth 290
   John 4, 115
   Mary 4
   Norman 115
   Norman 290, 334
Armstrong
   Agatha 81
   John 81

Ashburn
   Betty 99
   Edward 416
   Haynie 397
   Sally 99
   William 397
   William 18, 99
Astain/Astin
   George 60, 169, 240, 248
   John 27
   Valentine 27
   William 27

Bailey
   Charles 283
   Daniel 280
   Mary 283
   William 280
Ball
   Joseph 19, 178
   Luke 398
   William 177
Balvard
   Robert 53, 66
Barker
   William 419
Barns
   Edward 93
   Edwin 305
   Henry 91
   James 93
Barrett/Barrott
   Charles 118
   Edward 45
   Jane 31
   Nathaniel 45
   William 31

Bartes
    George 275
    Hannah 275
Baysie
    William 33
Beachem
    Isaac 11, 16
Bean/Beane
    George 323
    George Y. 385
    John 196
    Peter 90, 98, 232, 279, 280
Bearman
    John 431
Bee
    Shaderick 355
Bell
    Anne 9
    Cynor 350
    William 350
    William 9
Belvard
    Robert 78, 92, 125
Benn
    Arthur 258
    Whiden 258
Bennet/Bennett
    Fielding 107, 108
    Richard 310, 313
    Robert 108
Berry
    Mary 6
    Patience 3
    Thomas 3, 6
    William 3

Betts
    Betty 331
    Charles 114, 115, 173, 216, 235
    Elizabeth 331
    George 216, 235
    John 115, 173
    John 216, 251
    Jordan 267
    Jordan 309
    Thomas 26
    William 114
Bickerdick
    Major 193
Black
    Robert 324
Blackerby
    Grig Glascock 323
    Thomas Gascock 336
Blackwell
    William 171, 172
Blanch
    Ezekiel 261
Blincoe
    Ann 76
    James 76, 188
    Joanne 165
    John 15, 165
    Thomas 96
    William 188
Blueford/Bluford
    Elijah 339
    James 360
    Jane 339
Blundell
    Judith 104
Boggess
    Bennett 21
    Giles 21
Boush
    Bennett 305
Bowes
    Richard 152

Bradger
 John 341
 Thomas 341
 William 341
Brann
 Vincent 388
Bridgman
 Joseph 106
 Joseph 106
 Rodham 360
 William 360
Brin/Brinn
 Becky 340
 Griffin 319
 Joshua 319
 Peggy 340
 Winny 340
Brown
 Charles 297
 George 349
 John 161
 Joseph 349
 Manly 2
 Thomas 297
 Thomas 2, 93, 297
 William 161
Bryan
 John 390
Burk
 Ellen 380
 Thomas 378
Burress
 Elizabeth 412, 413
 William W. 412, 413
Burros
 Charles 164
 John 147, 148, 164
Burrows
 Charles 126
 John 126
Burton
 Richard 294, 312
 Thomas 312

Bush
 Betty 156
 Bibby 156
 Isaac 156
 John 156
 Susannah 156
Bussell
 Adam 213, 214
 Mathew 231, 252
 Phillip 231, 252
Butterfield
 Elizabeth 36

Cammell
 Thomas 269
Campbell
 Betty 332
 Elizabeth Dawson 332
 John 25
 William 88
Care
 Judy 28
 Thomas 28
Carrold
 Patrick 1
Carter
 Champion 389
 Charles 112
 Isaac 375
 James 394, 418
Carty
 Jane 15
 John 15
Cessaty
 John 357
Chapman
 Peter 37
Chilton
 Fleet 205
 Jesse 364
 John 205
 Judith 205
 Stephen 54, 56, 106, 205

Christy
- Charles 49
- George 49
- Mary 49
- Robert 49
- Sarah 49

Churchwell
- Sarahann Headen 36

Clark/Clarke
- Benjamin 205, 217, 257
- John 301
- William 295, 296
- ____ 301

Claughton
- Richard Jr. 137, 138
- William 362, 371

Coats
- Daniel 376
- George 179
- John 179
- Lavina 386

Cockrell
- John 39

Coffee
- Ezekiel 94, 124
- James 94

Coleman
- Charles 307
- Charles 306, 307
- William 306

Coles
- Edward 426

Collins
- Timothy 117
- William 117

Colman
- William 429

Colston
- Thomas 122, 123

Conway
- George 63
- John 32
- Peter Hack 63
- Robert 32

Cook/Cooke
- John 82
- William 125
- William 82, 125

Cookman
- John 424

Cooper
- Sampson 430
- Samuel 430

Coppedge
- Charles Jr. 120

Corbell
- Richard 104
- Stephen 355

Corbill
- John 426
- John 426

Cornish
- Hiram 402, 406
- John 135
- Juliet 401, 408
- Richard 135
- William 366, 401, 404
- William 366

Cotfield
- Ezekiel 52
- John 52

Cottrell
- Daniel 41, 56
- David 279
- John 41, 56
- John 279

Courtney
- James 206

Coward
- Fielding 143
- William 143

Cox
- John 14
- William 14

Crain/Craine
- James 268
- Rebecca 226
- Richard 268
- Stephen 239
- Stephen 239

Cralle
    John Jr. 192
    Rodham 207
    Rodham Kenner 207
Crowther
    James 254
    William 254
Crute
    Richard 21
Curtice
    Elizabeth 290
    George 99
    George 278, 290
    John 99
    Molly 325
    Nancy 325
    Rachel 325
    Thomas 278
Curtis
    George 177
    George 359
    John 177
    William 271

Dameron
    Anne 316
    Frances 316
    Hezekiah 356, 364
    Holland T. 374
    James 110
    Jeremiah 356, 364
    John 110, 316, 330
    Margaret 111
    Moses 111
    Richard Porter 110
    Roger 250
    Samuel 326
    Sarah 111
    William 110, 316
    William Jr. 110
Danks
    George 204
    George 149, 204, 226, 238
    John 238
    Mary 226
    William 149

Daugherty
    Cornelius 184
Davis
    Elizabeth 101
    Hiram, 399, 400
    John 101
    John 101, 105
    Joseph 105
    Robert 85
    Samuel 349, 354
Dawson
    John 215
    William Dameron 215
Day
    William 392
Dellsby
    Frances 178
Denny
    John 158
    John 158, 190
    William 190
Doolan
    Mary 25
Dowlin
    John 260
Drew
    Boatman 292
    John 291, 294
    Richard 294
Dudley
    Betty 271
Dunaway
    Abraham 314, 315, 320
    Anne 286
    Catherine 286
    Churchill 286
    Fortunas 187
    Joseph 286
    Mary 286
    William 395

Dyches/Dykes
    Eleanor 289
    John 263
    Pendly 263
    Richard 263
    Robert 263
    Thomas 263
    William 263

Edwards
    Daniel 331
    Elisha 331
    Ellen 331
    George 83
    Isaac 83
    John 83, 253
    Ralph 18
    Richard 244, 260, 304
    Robert 355
    Thomas 304
    William 18, 253, 331, 356
    William 331
Efferd/Efford
    John 62, 113
Ellicot
    Charles 316
Elmore
    John 132
    John H. 417
    Josiah 132
    Mary 372
Everitt
    Rawleigh 241
    William 241

Farned
    Edwin 164
Fitzmorris
    James 64
Fletcher
    George Waden 343, 346
Flynt
    John 73
    John 73, 222

Forrester
    Richard P. 410
    William W. 409, 410
Foster
    Benjamin 27
Foushee
    John 72
France/French
    John 162
    Rodham 162, 317
    Samuel 162, 340
    Shapleigh 162, 361
Frobus
    Hacka 355
    James 355

Gamewell
    John 65
    John 65
Garlington
    Christopher 186
    John 171, 172
    Joseph 186
    William 172
Garner
    Anne 303
    James 338
    James 42
    Jesse 42
    Jesse 292
    Parish 180, 181
    Richard 155
    Vincent 303
Gaskins
    Edwin 160
    John 85
    John 39, 85
    Josiah 251
    Josiah 160, 233
    Josias 115
    Josias 115
    Thomas 39, 233, 256, 265, 266
Gibson
    John 432

Gill
    Champion 355
    Ellis 111
    Thomas 111, 242
    Thomas 111, 242
    William 355
Gordan
    Baptist 62
Gordon
    Robert 317
Grayson
    William 207, 212
Greenstreet
    Richard 136
Greenwood
    William 420
Grinsted
    John 378
Groves
    George 389, 394

Hadaway
    William 42
Hadwell
    Jane 51
Hague
    Francis 89
    Hannah 89
    Joseph 89
Hall
    Alice Slack 260
    Astin 363
    Elizabeth 401, 405
    Francis 348
    John Jr. 247
    Martin 353
    Stephen 9
Hammertree
    Elisha Payne 329
Hammond
    Judith 129
    Peter 129

Harcum
    George 338
    Greek 355, 367
    James 176, 223, 243, 415
    Thomas 293
    Thomas 17, 223, 243
    Valentine 375
Hardee
    Mary 166
    Parrot 166
Harding
    Hopkins 119, 121
    John 37, 96
    Mark 66
    Mark 160, 197, 198, 270
    Thomas 270
    Thomas 37, 66, 96
Harford
    Alice 300
    Catesby 300
    Charles 300
    Charles Lovelace 305
    Mary 300
    William 300
Harper
    James 123
    John 19
    Joshua 122, 123
    Sarah 19
Harris
    Jesse 352
    John 352
Harrison
    James 22, 317, 361
    John 352
    Priscilla 182
    Thomas 48
    Thomas 22
Hart
    Robert 38
    William 38
Harvey
    James 30
    James 30
Hathaway
    Thomas 246

Hawkins
    William 317
Hayden
    Elizabeth 133
    Lewis 133
Haynie
    Abraham 222
    Bridgar 377
    Charles 11
    Charles 258
    George 45, 46, 102, 154, 163, 170, 230
    Isaac 412, 413
    Maximillian 222
    Ormsby 11
    Richard 288
    Sarah 46
    William 46
Headley
    Griffin 387
Headon
    Lewis 189
    William 189
Heath
    John 72
Hill
    Corbell 12
    Ezekiel 24
    James 5
    John 68, 90, 91
    John 90, 228, 308
    Luke 5, 12, 91
    Nanny 308
    Nicholas 228
    Spencer 236
    Spencer 236
    Sukil 68
    Thomas 24, 47
Hodges
    John 211
Hogan
    John 337
    John 337
    Thomas 337

Hopkins
    Betty 355
    John 355
Hornsby
    John 33, 34
    John 33, 188, 209, 229
Hudnall
    Joseph 255
    Joseph 318
    Richard 175
Hudson
    Abishae 299
    Fielding 295
    Keziah 295, 296
    Mary 296
    Robuck 102, 163
    Rodham 102
Hughlett
    Betty 379
    Ephrain 198
    John 198
    John 270
    Nicholas 198, 227
    Roger W. 327
    Samuel 80
    Thomas 232
    Winter 232
    Yarrot 227
Hughs
    William 307
Humphris
    George 368
    Hannah 368
    Jane 218, 318
Hunton
    John 201
Hurst
    Henry 53, 78
    John 53
Hutt
    Reid 167
    Thomas 167

Ingram
   Elijah 35
   Elizabeth 35
   Hiram 397

James
   Charles 22, 94, 124
   Daniel 118
   Hugh 179
   John 24
   Thomas 118

Jaques
   Thomas 393

Johnston
   William 30

Johnstone
   James 151
   Thomas 151
   Thomas 151
   William 151

Jones
   Armistead 385, 387
   Catesby 362
   George 382
   Griffin 381
   Hannah 387
   John 154
   Joseph 397
   R.H. 425
   Samuel 360
   Solomon 109
   Thomas 282
   Walter 109
   William 154
   Winney 397

Keiser
   Ferdinand 421
   Frances 421
   Frederick 421
   Polly 421

Kellem
   Richard 197
   Richard 197

Kenner
   Francis 231
   John William Hicks 75
   William 75
   Winder 274

Kent
   Charles 308
   John 308

Kern
   James 373

Kessady
   John 365

Kesterson
   Sarah 140
   William 140

King
   John 361
   Thaddeus 416
   William 361
   William Davy 416

Kirk
   George 119
   Isaac 119
   John 135

Lackey
   John T. 409, 410, 415

Lamkin
   Jane 13

Lancaster
   John 105

Lansdell
   Benjamin 384

Lawler
   James 145
   Nicholas 145

Lawless
   James 40
   Nicholas 40

Leach
   John 84, 287
   Judith 150
   William 84, 287

Lealand
   John 180, 181
   Peter 181

Lee
    Hugh 427
Leland
    Haynie 359
    John 180
Lewis
    James 233, 256, 265, 266
    John 380
Lock
    John 82
Lowry
    John 359
    Peggy 359
    Sally 359
    William 276
    William 276
Lucas
    Sally 369
    Samuel 369
    Thomas 369
    William 369
Lunsford
    Edwin 98
    John 88
    Samuel 330
    Swanson 98
    William 6

Mahanes
    Samuel 20
Malady
    John 199, 200, 213, 214
Maley
    John 381
Marsh
    Gideon 343
    John 210
    Peter 210
    Thomas 210
Martin
    James 421

Mason
    Alice 67
    Betty 370, 372
    Eli 321
    Eli 370, 372
    James 199, 200, 325
    Jane 67
    Judith 67
    Peter 67, 321
Mathews
    Moses 176
Mayden
    John 57
    Tabytha 57
Mayes
    Christopher 136
    John 136
Mays
    Henry 7
    Susanna 7
McCall
    George 63
McCalley
    Charles 153
    Charles 153
    Hannah 192
    John 153, 155, 168, 192
McCoy
    Daniel 220, 221
McGoon
    John 4, 74, 247
    William 247
Miller
    Robert 225
Mills
    Jane 245
Mitchell
    Frederick 390
Molony
    Michael 211
    Michael 211
Moltimore
    Samuel 347

Moore
    Charles 398
    Elijah 392
    Richard 398
Morriss
    John 116
Morton
    William 149, 204, 237, 267, 302, 303
Mott
    Isaac 127, 128
    Isaac 366, 367
    John 97
    Mosely 170
    Mosely 170
    Mosly 97
    Randal 128
    Randolph 59
    Randolph 59, 127, 173, 190, 191, 202, 220, 221, 235, 239, 241, 253, 273
    William 69, 70, 97, 114, 146
Murphey/Murphy
    Darby 183
    John 71
    Joshua 25
    William 183
    William 71

Nash
    Jemimah 8
    Robert 8
Neale
    Christopher 337
    John 333
    Rody 337
Neasome
    John 195
Nelms
    Aaron 121
    Aaron 115, 121, 209
    Meredith 209
    Spenser 115
Newsome
    Epap^a 187
    John 187

Nicken/Nickens
    Baldwin 411
    Betsy 421
    Emily 421
    William 421
Nutt
    Benjamin 193
    Farnefold 144
    Farnifold 194
    James 193
    John 144
    John 144
    Thomas 194

Ober
    Henry 254
Oldham
    Elizabeth 311
    James 277, 331
    John Jr. 26
    Lucy Fleming 182
Owens
    George 355
    Hugh 360

Palmer
    Daniel 288
    James 134
    John 134
    Joshua 50
    Lott 234
    Nargail 234
    Nargail Sharezar 288
    Robert 5
    Thomas 234
Parker
    Mary 137, 157
    Thomas 137, 157
    Thomas Turner 353
Parry
    John 29
Patridge
    John 25
Patton
    John 407, 408

Pendergrass
    John 55
Perie
    Andrew 427
    Jane 427
Phillips
    George 104
Pickering
    George 399, 400
Pickrell
    Isaac 316
Pickren
    George 360
    George 28
    Heli 355
    John 334
    Orange 334, 393
Pierson
    William 381
Piper
    David 338
Pitman
    Burgess 342
    Darcus 244
    Fortunatus 342
    Jesse 203
    Joseph 244
    William 47
Place
    John 432
Popewell
    John H. 359
Poplar
    Betty 331
Popperwell
    Sally 311
Popwell
    Sarah 316
Porter
    Betty 330
    Richard 330
Potts
    Enoch 322
Pritchard
    Swan 48

Prosser
    William 312, 321, 350
Pugh
    Elizabeth 51
    Thomas 51
Pullen
    Thomas 68

Railey
    Daniel 29
    Mary 284
    Sarah 284
    Winefred 29
Reason
    Margaret 195
    Nancy 244
Redman
    Polly 355
Rice
    Isaac 278
    William 397
Richardson
    Isaac 159
    Jesse 317
Ricks
    Daniel 371
Riveer
    James 281
Roberts
    Giles 185
    Giles 184, 185
    James 184
    Rebecca 185
Robertson
    Henry 152
Robinson
    George 332
    Thomas 72
    Thomas 72
Robuck
    John 268
    William 268
Rochester
    William 391

Rock
    Alexander 405
    Frances 403, 404
    Thomas 411
    William 406, 416
Rogers
    Edward 54
    George 54
Roles
    Francis 142, 147
Rolls
    Francis 126
Routt
    Anthony Sydnor 310
    William 362
Rowt
    John 113
    Richard 113
    William 113
Rust
    George 283
Rylie
    Thomas 328

Sampson
    Lewis 351
Sank
    John 396, 414
Schofield
    Betty 269
Sebastian
    Henage 240, 248
    Joseph 240
Sebree/Sebrie/Seebrie
    Catherine 298
    Elizabeth 298
    George 298
    John 169
    John 10, 169, 191, 264
    Nancy 191
    Richard 298
    Sinah 175
    William 1, 298
Self
    Ewell 313
    Henry 313

Shaw
    Walter 363
Shearman
    Martin 272
    Martin Jr. 186, 208
Shiverill
    Allen Long 143
Short
    Nancy 244
    Patty 260
Smith
    Benjamin O. 388
    Betty 229
    Diane 17
    James M. 399, 400
    John 229
    John 2
    Samuel 17
    Thomas 223, 252
Smither
    George 58
    George 58, 117, 219, 243, 269, 271
    John 347
    John 228
    William 238, 383
Snead
    James A. 419, 420
Snow
    Elisha 14
    William 390
Spriggs
    Joseph 335, 344
    Joseph 344
Spry
    Betty 274
    James 274
Straughan
    David 212
    John 212
    John C. 376

Sullivan/Sullivant
   Chloe 95
   Cornelious 95, 196
   Cornelious 95, 112, 262
   Dennis 95, 112
   Jesse 95
   Nancy 95
   Robert 418
   Thomas 95, 262
Summers
   John 138
   William 138
Summors
   John 250
Sutton
   James 92
   John 236
   Thomas 259
   William 92
Swanson
   Chloe 61
   Dennis 356
   Dennis 52
   John 61
   William 356
   Willis 356
Swift
   William 38
Sydnor
   Epaphroditus 208
   Giles 208

Talley
   John 44
   John 44
Taylor
   John 51
   John Jr. 8
   Michael 225
   Thomas 365
Tellus
   John 282
   Rodham 282
Templeman
   James 115, 273
   Samuel 273

Thomas
   Aggy 264
   Amey 377
   Bill 377
   George 202
   Harriet 425
   James 264
   Job 382
   John 382
   John 291
   Peter 281
   Richard 16
   Richard 16, 202, 255
   Rodham 281
   Spencer 379
   Susanna 317
   Thomas 314, 315, 320
   Thurston 425
   William 25
   William S. 354
Thompson
   John 423
   Lucretia 43
   Osbern 423
   Richard 43, 132, 167, 183
   Sophia 423
   William 423
   Winnefred 43
Thomson
   Richard 109
Thornton
   Stewart Warren 348
Tignor
   Sally 355
Tillery
   George 77
   George 77
   Thomas 77
Timberlake
   Ep^a 246
Todd
   Cornelius 74
   Cornelius 23, 74
   William 23

Tossett
   Richard 10
   Richard 10
Toulson
   William 389
Tousend/Townsend
   Haynie 146
   John 141
   Soloman 174
   William 146
Trap/Trop
   Letty 131
   Moses 131, 139
   Nancy 139
   William 355
Travers
   Henry 373
Trussell
   John 159
   Rodham 159
Tulles/Tullis
   John 206, 230
   Rodham 206, 230
Turner
   Benjamin 386
   Charles B. 423
   Thomas 328
Tycer
   Jemima 80
   Richard 80

Vanlandingham
   Anne 13
   Benjamin Jr. 103
   Joseph 417
   Susanna 13
   William 381
Venie
   Cyrus 383
Vibratt
   Lancelot 103
   Thomas 103

Wagstaff
   Nancy 359

Walker
   James 217, 257
   John 429
   John 217, 218, 224, 285, 318
   Mary 142, 147
   Molly 224
   Thomas 285
   Thomas 224
   William 429
   Winefred 218, 318
Warrick
   Alice 100
   Richard 100
Waters
   Robert 130
Watkins
   Brenet 422
Watts
   Richard 84
Way
   John 302, 309
   Richard 302, 309
Weaver
   Elijah 384
   Mary 249
Webb
   ____ 50
   George 219
   James 203, 272
   James 203
   John 259
   Joseph 272
   Moses 50
   Tarpley 244
   William 120
   William 120, 219
Weekes
   Walter 428
Wells
   Thaddeus 391
West
   Leroy 168
   Lucy 182
White
   Hannah 431
   Richard 431

Wiggen
    John 327
Wilday
    Frederick 237
    William 237
Wildy
    William 368
Wilkins
    Catherine 87, 277
    James Fontain 79, 116
    John 87
    John 55, 134, 277
    Mary Ann Baylis 345
    Peter 87, 99, 263
    Thomas 263
    Thomas 79, 87, 99, 116
    William 87
Williams
    Butler 276
    Griffith 71
    John 374
    John 86, 188
    Thomas 275
    Vincent 188
Wilson
    Joseph 394
    Nathaniel 245
Winstead
    Lucius S. 414
Winter
    John 201
    William 201
Wood
    John 7, 77
    William 77
Woodcock
    John S. 189
Wright
    Thomas 60
    Winfield 60

Yapp/Yopp
    John 58, 59, 73
Yeates
    Francis 141

Yost
    Hiram 395
    Hiram N. 394

Parents of
Apprentices Not Named

Blincoe
    James 76
Dellsby
    Frances 178
Fitzmorris
    James 64
Mahane
    Samuel 20
Miller
    Robert 225
Potts
    Enoch 322
Taylor
    Michael 225

No Surnames for Following
Apprentices

_____
Adam 381
_____
Amanda 424
_____
Harriet 381

www.ingramcontent.com/pod-product-compliance
Lightning Source LLC
Chambersburg PA
CBHW070255100426
42743CB00011B/2246